WHAT KIND OF RESULTS CAN YOU EXPECT FROM DAN'S NO B.S. SALES SUCCESS STRATEGIES?

"In 1978, I went to work as a sales  that sold hand-held pricing equipment to ret to General Manager, but saw wit business was endangered. Althoug and I bought the company, it wasn Dan Kennedy, that I really discovered how to make my business the leader in its industry. **Using Dan's methods—including many in this book—my business grew from $3.5-million in sales in 1991 to $13.4-million in 2006, and, while our sales increased 4-fold, our profits multiplied 8-fold."**

—Keith Lee, American Retail Supply

"I've had your *No B.S. Sales Success* book in my possession for only three days. I have set up eight presentations, closed two deals . . . **the first presentation 'the Kennedy way' went off without a hitch—they were pre-sold before I arrived, and that order put $13,475.00 profit in my pocket."**

—Tom Halloran, Medical Supplies

"I have just returned from a trade show that was almost cancelled because of low registration. As I prepared, I re-adjusted and remembered your admonition that it is the *quality* of the prospects, not the quantity. As I left the show having **written five large orders, reaching our goal,** the organizer of the show—who had struggled to satisfy the other exhibitors—said 'You're my success story.' My success is related to what you say in your book about selling in difficult conditions, when others can't. "

—Lisa Wilgus

"I am writing with a long overdue 'thank you' for everything you have done for my business and personal life. I have read all your books repeatedly . . . I have used your strategies to **triple the size of my family's insurance agency in the past 36 months . . . from $3.4-million to $10.5-million**. We are now able to dominate our target markets regardless of the economy or competition.

—Michael McLean, McLeanInsuranceLive.com

"I have lived and worked in Australia, slugged it out, on the street selling, to make a living. I knew there had to be an easier way, and I looked and looked for 25 years. When I found Dan Kennedy and adapted his unique way, my business took off like a cat on a hot tin roof in the outback. This year alone, Dan Kennedy was responsible for **adding more than one million dollars to my income**—and I never spoke to him!"

—Ed Burton, Financial/Investment/Asset Protection Advisor, Sydney, Australia

"My current success is entirely YOUR fault. I thank you so much. Changed my life. I'm not exaggerating. Your *No B.S. Sales Success* book is the #1 reason behind my success. I was born a big baby, 11.5 pounds, to a petite woman, my legs and feet grew crookedly insider her womb, and I had to wear special braces from birth to age 3 to straighten them out. My perfectionist father viewed me as a failure, according to the family, began drinking heavily after my birth, so I grew up with an alcoholic father. I feared rejection immensely, and practically lived inside my bedroom, hidden away from my father and the rest of the world as much as possible. I actually forced myself into sales to try and conquer my fears but I failed miserably, even declaring bankruptcy at age 21. I tried selling everything: cars, vacuum cleaners, insurance, you name it. **One day I came across your book. One statement made in it changed my whole career: 'positioning, not prospecting.'**

"With guidance from your book, I specialized in a niche, I became an expert, I used my writing skills to create lead generation ads and free reports, and began attracting pre-qualified prospects to me so I no longer had to prospect or ever feel rejected. I subsequently **became THE top selling representative at a Fortune 500 company.** Today, I've become a highly paid copywriter, selling via ads and sales letters. Thank you Dan, for everything."

—Michel Fortin, Ottawa, Ontario, Canada, www.SuccessDoctor.com

N◎ B.S.

SALES
SUCCESS

IN THE
NEW
ECONOMY

- Meet the New Economy Customer
- Master 15 Trust-Building Sales Strategies
- Get Past Any "No"

Dan S. Kennedy

EP
Entrepreneur.
Press

Publisher: Jere L. Calmes
Cover Design: David Shaw
Production and Composition: Eliot House Productions

This publication is designed to provide accurate and authoritative information in regard to the subject matter covered. It is sold with the understanding that the publisher is not engaged in rendering legal, accounting or
other professional services. If legal advice or other expert assistance is
required, the services of a competent professional person should be sought.

Library of Congress Cataloging-in-Publication Data
  Kennedy, Dan S., 1954–
    No bs sales success for the new economy/by Dan Kennedy
      p.   cm.
    Includes bibliographical references.
    ISBN-10: 1-59918-357-9 (alk. paper)
    ISBN-13: 978-1-59918-357-2 (alk. paper)
    1. Selling. 2. Success in business. I. Title.
  HF5438.25.K4728 2009
  658.85—dc22   2009010904

Printed in Canada
14 13 12 11 10 09   10 9 8 7 6 5 4 3 2 1

The old economy is shattered and gone forever.

It's never coming back as it was.

While some time-honored, reliable business strategies and skills continue to have their place—are even more important than ever— they must be combined with new, more sophisticated, more disciplined methods in sync with the realities of the New Economy and the psychology of its consumers and clients.

Welcome to The New Economy

Well, it's not like we shouldn't have seen this coming.

Problem: We are monstrously over-stored. The same stores every few miles. The joke about Starbucks was it had reached the point they were opening new Starbucks in the Men's Rooms in existing Starbucks. Me-too, same-as, indistinguishable chain stores, chain restaurants with zero differentiation right across the parking lot from one another. Simply, much, much more than the market could support. Implosion certain destiny.

Problem: There are far too many over-lapping brands. Should there ever have been Cadillac pick-up trucks when GM also has Chevy and GMC trucks? Other than to perpetuate jobs locked in by union contract, could the existence of Pontiac *and* Buick *and* Chevy *and* Cadillac *and* GMC possibly be justified? Not unique to GM, though. Many other companies sinned similarly. And it seems everybody wanted to play in everybody else's sandbox, sacrificing their very identities to their detriment. Starbucks added egg, cheese, and meat breakfast sandwiches (that ruined the coffee aroma in their stores) while McDonalds hurried to add lattes and gourmet coffee while Subway added pizza while Dominos Pizza added sub sandwiches, your pharmacy added clothes and lawn furniture, Wal-Mart added iPhones. It's a damn mess. That must be cleaned up.

Problem: Everybody already owns too much stuff. How many cars, TVs, computers, games, remodeled kitchens, backyard decks can consumers consume before they need a break? Above all else, the recession was made and extended by demand problems.

Problem: Worst of all, salesmanship perished and service went to hell in a handbasket, as free-flowing, easy, excess credit and the latest in a series of fools' bubbles (this one with theoretically never-ending multiplying of property values so homes became ATM's, not invest-ments) enabled countless companies with poor sales practices, lazy and inept salespeople, sloppy over-staffing, casual management and abysmal customer service to prosper, or at least seem to prosper. Truth is, consumers welcomed a good excuse to stay home and stop buying and *punish*.

Imagine a very loosely held together, giant ball of yarn with dozens of loose ends poking out all over the place. It wouldn't matter much which of the loose ends you gave a good tug; the entire ball, really just a pile of yarn, would implode and collapse and unravel. So it has been with the economy. It really wouldn't have mattered if it had been too many sub-prime mortgages issued to poorly qualified and irresponsible borrowers, based on inflated equity with no regard to the borrowers' ability to pay, then bundled together in inventive investment packages or if it had been sudden skyrocketing of gas prices or if it had been the weight of mass-multiplied, poorly regulated hedge funds or accelerating disappearance of old-style manufacturing jobs sent overseas or just about any other loose end you might name—any one given a good yank would have been enough. Of course, when several got pulled hard in different directions at the same time . . . .

Incidentally, the real estate bubble was visible far, far in advance of its bursting. In 2003, an outstanding book on the subject, *The Coming Crash in the Housing Market* by John Talbott, a former vice president at Goldman Sachs and real estate economist, very accurately predict-ed both the mortgage meltdown and real estate crash we've recently experienced—and reading it saved me some money. Authoritative arti-cles began appearing pretty frequently from 2004 on, like the one on

July 26, 2004, in the *Financial Times*, headlined "Party Over—Turn Off the Housing Boom Lights," that stated that "the end is near in use of exotic type mortgage money." We should have seen this coming. Some of us did. I began foretelling in earnest of 2007–2008 in my *No B.S. Marketing Letter* and other publications in 2004.

What has been painfully revealed are extreme, systemic weaknesses and flaws and vulnerabilities—and gross excesses—throughout our socio-economic, financial, and political systems, papered over for a while, but worsening like undiagnosed disease all the while until, finally, we got slapped in the face with a monster recession. It's not my first rodeo. I built my first businesses during the Jimmy Carter recession, with tight credit, double-digit interest and inflation and unemployment rates, and gas shortages and gas lines. These things may very well be avoidable, but these things happen. For people seeing it firsthand for the first time it is terrifying and can be paralyz-ing. But it's not the first time and it won't be the last time traumatic change has replaced an old economy with a New Economy.

From Monster Recession to New Economy

For people who respond boldly, creatively, intelligently, and responsi-bly, grand and glorious new opportunities, greater in scope, more powerful for rapid wealth creation, and more accessible to all are being presented by the emerging New Economy. With honest Darwinism, the herds are being thinned, the weakest eaten, and the strongest stepping over carcasses in the street en-route to bigger and better things. You choose whether to lie down and be stepped on or to move forward—quickly—because moving forward is the only way not to be stepped on. The once generous and cheery economy is going through a very irritable and unforgiving mood. Conditions are harsh.

There are new opportunities. They have new requirements. There are also evergreen, time-honored, wholly reliable success principles most business owners and entrepreneurs have drifted from, neglected, or forgotten that must be restored as governing priorities. This book, *No B.S. Sales Success for the New Economy*, and its brother *No B.S. Business Success for the New Economy* are about all of those things: new opportunities, new requirements, neglected principles to be restored.

Let me briefly describe the emerging New Economy as it directly affects sales professionals. Here are the new realities:

1. All the power has returned to the customer and he knows he has it.

2. The customer's tolerance for anything ordinary—ordinary products, services, expertise, experiences, for the banal and commonplace, and certainly for incompetence—is zero.

3. Money will be spent more judiciously, so it will be available only to sales pros with a much higher level of knowledge, skill, preparation, discipline, and sophistication. A more cautious consumer, striving to be sensible and responsible, will be judging you and trying to determine if you are worthy of his trust before he buys from you. You will be under greater scrutiny.

4. You must genuinely earn your right to your customers' interest and support by providing well-matched, specialized, even customized product, service, and value propositions. People now have the opportunity, power, and awareness to demand what is specifically for them and precisely matched to their needs, interests, and desires. They are not going to be on buying sprees, buying whatever is in your wagon that you want to sell.

Contents

PART III

**A NO B.S. START-TO-FINISH
STRUCTURE FOR THE SALE**

PART IV

DUMB AND DUMBER: THINGS THAT
SABOTAGE SALES SUCCESS

PART V

MY BIGGEST SECRET TO
EXCEPTIONAL RESULTS IN SELLING:
TAKEAWAY SELLING

PART VI

REFERENCE SECTION

FOREWORD

from the previous edition
By America's #1 Sales Trainer,
TOM HOPKINS

*E*very person who has chosen selling as a career must focus on getting the brass ring with every new contact they make. The brass ring for a salesperson is the closed sale. It's hearing the words "yes," "we'll take it," or "how soon can it be delivered/installed/set up?" Those words, and a check, credit card, or purchase order to go with them, validate the salesperson. They demonstrate in both physical actions and words that the salesperson is representing something of value to the client—so much value that the client is willing to exchange their security (spelled M-O-N-E-Y) for it. It also demonstrates that the salesperson did a good job, using their skills and talents in presenting the product in such a way that the client saw how the benefits it would provide fulfilled a need. Having a client say, "thank you" tells you they're happy the salesperson brought it their way. That "thank you" is like getting a standing ovation.

There's a lot of psychology behind what works and doesn't work in selling. It has to do with mind-sets (both yours and the client's), attitude, fears, perception, body language, voice, vocabulary, style, grooming, expectations, preparation, and too many other aspects to list here. An entire encyclopedia of selling could be written if every little nuance of selling was to be taught. It might take you a few years to read such a series of books.

My questions to you is, do you want to take the course in psychology to understand what's behind the sales process, or do you just want to hear what works? If you're like most salespeople, you're looking for the shortest route between where you are now and increased sales. That's the benefit of this book. Dan has literally eliminated the B.S. in explaining great ways to make more sales.

We can learn many things simply by reading, but we only benefit if we invest time in thinking about what we've read and how it applies to what we're doing. We excel when we put the knowledge gained to use. This is a relatively short book. Invest your time wisely in reading it with thoughtfulness of how you can apply the strategies it contains. You'll be glad you did.

—Tom Hopkins

Tom Hopkins is world-renowned as a master sales trainer. For more information contact him at info@tomhopkins.com. Receive free sales content, tips, and closes by subscribing to Tom's selling skills e-newsletter at www.tomhopkins.com.

PREFACE

T here are basically four types of salespeople: sales professionals with strong ambition who are eager to strengthen and fine-tune their skills; sales professionals who are jaded, close-minded, cynical, and stuck; nonsalespeople who realize they need to be salespeople, such as doctors, auto repair shop owners, carpet cleaners; *non*salespeople who either do not recognize they need to be or are resistant to the idea.

In The NEW ECONOMY, only the most self-aware, self-disciplined, and highly skilled salespeople who view their selling as art and science, as a professional skill, and as a sophisticated process will prosper. During the purge beginning in earnest in 2008, some sales professions quickly lost from 25% to 50% of their entire populations, and many will never return to their peak sizes. Some business categories mirrored this shrinkage. You would think this ratio of fewer providers and sellers to the growing consumer population might permit less skillful and diligent salespeople to prosper, but the opposite is true; the consumer knows the power has shifted to him and has no intention of returning it to undeserving hands. Placing yourself in the proper mind-set space here is predictive of your future prosperity in or forced exit from your business.

Ambitious Salespeople 1	Stuck Salespeople
3 Nonsalespeople Eager to Learn	4 Resistant Nonsalespeople

Historically, this book has resonated with those in the first and third quadrant. Wasted on the others. I've spent more than one-quarter of an entire lifetime, over 30 years, working with people in both the first and third quadrant. And doing my level best to avoid the folks in the second and fourth. In The New Economy, it's easier to avoid them because their populations are thinning rapidly. The first and third categories are dominating and will dominate, and all the income is going to move to them. In the old economy, the income divided, in a sales field, roughly 20% to the 80% of the population I'd define as Stuck Salespeople, 80% to the 20% of the group working as Ambitious Salespeople. Same in business: 80% of the money to business owners who might never define themselves as sales professionals but who were nevertheless eager to learn and use smart selling strategies—about 20% of the population. That looked like this:

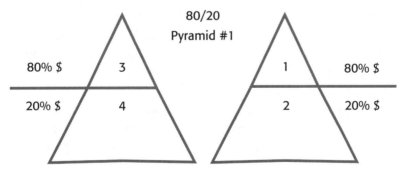

In The New Economy, 95% of the money gravitates to the Ambitious and Eager-to-Learn, and will separate and be shared disproportionately by the most ambitious and most eager. It is now essential to be smarter, sharper, more progressive, more aggressive, more organized . . . more "everything" in order to get to the top of this new pyramid, which looks like this.

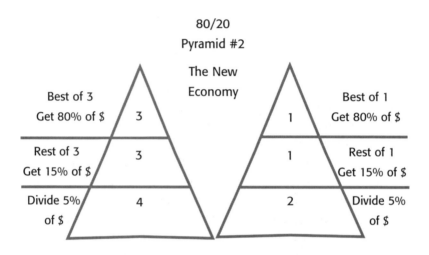

80/20
Pyramid #2

Incidentally, I'm cheered by all this. I detest salespeople and businesspeople who coast, who are intellectually lazy, who perform half-heartedly, who expect high rewards for low effort, and hope to see them starved out altogether. Rather than redistributing success to a broader swath of the business owner and sales professional populations in some socialist-leaning ideal of equality, I'm happy to see the success concentrated into the hands of a smaller-than-ever minority of people who choose to make themselves exceptional and exceptionally deserving. To the rest, I say: let them eat crumbs.

This is a book intended to equip you to gain membership in—and keep membership in—that elite fraternity enjoying the top incomes, the greatest security, the most independence and power, and the highest status. If that is not where you sincerely, sincerely, sincerely want to be, it will be wasted on you; may be too blunt and direct and "No B.S." for you; may suggest an "accept nothing less than the sale made" attitude you'll find predatory or militaristic, that you just won't *like*. If you prefer a more mamby-pampby approach, the bookstore shelves are full of books on selling featuring just that—feel free to trade this in. But if you want to be at the top of The New Economy and are willing to do whatever is required to be there, this *is* the book for you.

This book summarizes the most important strategies I've developed over my 30 years—some originating from my own experience, some originating from my observation of super-successful sales pros' behaviors, then converted to replicable strategy, and all honed to perfection by my high six-figure and seven-figure earning clients I coach, and top sales companies I devise strategies for. These trustworthy strategies are placed in the context of The New Economy and its demands.

There are a great many things this book is NOT. It is NOT, for example, a textbook approach to selling. It is not about moral or spiritual philosophy (those matters are left to you). It is notice-ably free of trendy new terminology, buzzwords, and psycho-babble so many sales trainers and authors seem to be fond of. And it is not a motivational book either. If you need someone else to motivate you, you have far bigger problems than this book might tackle. Or any hundred books, for that matter.

This is simply, a straightforward, relentlessly pragmatic, "no b.s." presentation of what REALLY works in selling.

Not what *should* work. Not the academic theories about sell-ing. What REALLY works.

You may not thoroughly enjoy this book. It may make you uncomfortable. Confronting, challenging, and rethinking long-held beliefs and habits is provocative and often profitable, but rarely comfortable or enjoyable. But you can trust this book.

My aim is very simple: after reading this book, I intend for you to implement behavioral and procedural changes that will immediately and dramatically increase the income you earn from selling. This book is all about putting more money in your pocket, nothing loftier than that, nothing less than that. And if we have to break a few eggs to make that omelet, then that's what we'll do.

You might want to know, this book has had a former life and a long life. It was first published in 1994, continuously through 1996, a 2nd edition published in 1999, then in print through 2001, then a thoroughly updated and substantially expanded new edition was published in 2004. Of course, a whole lot happened between 2004 and 2009. A tumultuous five years. And those changes manufacturing The New Economy required yet another update of this book. But why is it important for you to know you've wound up with "the sales book that will not die" in your hands? Two reasons. First, as evidence you've gotten your paws on strategies that ARE really valuable and that DO really work. Successful salespeople recommend this book to each other, they stream to the bookstores, demand it, and even when a publisher has lost interest in it, the marketplace has insisted it be put back onto the store shelves. (By the way, now you can tell others about this book by sending them to www.nobsbooks.com, to get free excerpts. And you will find additional resources and support material for the book as well as previews of my other books—even free, view-on-demand videos—there as well.) Anyway, second, no matter its most recent updating, you will still be able to find references in the book that are obviously dated, or references to my writing of its first or prior editions, and I didn't want you to be confused by that, thus this explanation. Given the time lapse between writing and publishing, it's impossible for a book to be perfectly current. Furthermore, great object lessons should continue being told, however much time has passed.

Now, to the important stuff: quick, practical actions you can take, to make selling easier, less stressful, more fun, and much, much more lucrative and rewarding.

About the Structure of This Book

This book is divided into five parts. In PART I, I describe the 15 strategies that I use most in selling. Each is a stand-alone application and any one of them alone could significantly improve your results in selling. But they can also be linked together differently for different situations for increased value and power.

In PART II, I deal with what goes on before selling can even begin: finding, attracting, and getting into a desirable selling situation with a prospect. As you'll see, I'm no fan of the way most salespeople carry out this job. Here you'll discover some rather radical ideas.

In PART III, I provide a framework for selling. The various pieces described in PARTS I and II can be plugged in and out of this structure.

In PART IV, I share with you the dumbest things salespeople do to sabotage themselves.

In PART V, I reveal my personal best, most valued, contrary approach to selling. It may not be for everybody; it may not be for you. Frankly, I argued with myself about putting it in or leaving it out. I ultimately decided I would not be playing fair with you if I sold you a book about selling and held back the information most responsible for my own success. Use it as you will, and good luck.

—Dan Kennedy

Important Notices

1. **For anyone who is gender or political-correctness sensitive:** I have predominately used *he, him,* etc. throughout the book with only occasional exception, rather than awkwardly saying *he or she, him or her*. I do not mean this as a slight to women, only as a convenience. I am not getting paid by the word.

2. **To clarify some terminology:** throughout the book you will see me refer to some of the people used in the examples as Members. That means they are Members of Glazer-Kennedy Insider's Circle™ the international organization of entrepreneurs, business owners, and sales professionals receiving my monthly *No B.S. Marketing Letter,* monthly *Marketing Gold* audio CD, other publications and benefits depending on membership level, and possibly participating in local Chapters and Kennedy Study Groups. You can "test drive" membership yourself, free of fee, with the Free Gift Offer on page 260.

   You will also see me refer to some as Private Clients or as Platinum Members. All are Glazer-Kennedy Insider's Circle™ Members but may also be in consulting relationships or in my private business coaching group.

PART I

15 NO B.S. STRATEGIES

FOR EXCEPTIONAL SUCCESS IN
SALES, PERSUASION, AND
NEGOTIATIONS

CHAPTER 1

STRATEGY 1
IMMUNITY TO THE
WORD "NO"

My first sales position (and the only time I've been employed by someone else) was a wonderful training ground. I learned a lot from my experiences in that position, and you'll notice throughout this book that I refer to it several times. I now have nostalgia for these experiences, warm feelings for them that I, of course, did not have when living them. The ones I choose to write about in this book are not just "war stories" told because they are good or amusing stories—these are experiences that had lasting impact and have colored my strategic approach to advertising, marketing, and selling for more than 30 years and continue doing so today. They are not diminished in significance by age at all. In fact, I find them more relevant to The New Economy.

I was so wet-behind-the-ears I dripped when I was hired as the central states sales representative for a Los Angeles-based book publisher. I was assigned Ohio, Kentucky, Indiana, Michigan, and Pennsylvania. My job was to call on all the bookstores, department store book departments, discount stores, gift shops, and other retailers in that territory to service existing accounts and open new ones. Most of the company's books were humorous, impulse-purchase items. In many stores, the line of books was merchandised on the publisher's six-foot-high spinner racks, which I had to inventory and stock.

One minor fact that was not discussed when I was hired was that my territory had been "orphaned," and the established accounts had received no service of any kind for eight months or longer. I soon discovered that some of the customers were *a trifle* annoyed at having been sold this line of merchandise, promised service, and then ignored.

I was furnished with a computer printout of all the accounts and their purchase history. The first one I visited, a drugstore, provided a clue that things might not be well. I walked up to the owner, introduced myself as the new representative from the company, and watched a mild-mannered pharmacist turn into a raving lunatic. He grabbed me by the arm and dragged me into the back room where he showed me a pile of rack parts that had been shipped in, but that he had been unable to assemble. Surrounding that mess was a stack of boxes full of books. He told me that he had been invoiced for books and racks and had been dunned by a collector for payment, even though he had never had a chance to get the books on the floor to sell. He literally threw the rack parts out of the back door while screaming at me to take it all away.

In the next few weeks, I met with similar antagonism at almost every account I called on. I took a lot of racks and a lot of inventory out of stores. Besides being generally unpleasant and occasionally hazardous to my health, this situation was an economic disaster. I was being rated as a sales rep, and my bonuses were based on a "positive sales ratio" for the month. That means: sales less returns equal net sales.

The way I was going, I would have a negative sales figure for my first month—maybe my first year. **I determined that something had to change, and I had to be the one to create the change.**

That decision alone is an important tip about getting your own way. It doesn't much matter whether we're talking about selling, like the work I was doing, or negotiating business deals, or running a business. Anybody can look good and get good results when everybody else is cooperating and everything is going as it is supposed to. Under those conditions, just about anybody can have a good time and make a lot of money. And that is exactly what was happening, during the extended economic boom commencing with Ronald Reagan's re-engineering of the near-Depression economy made by Jimmy Carter all the way through to President Bush #2, who, incidentally, presided over a record-breaking 55 consecutive months of job growth in this country, stock market rising to record highs, and all the rest. People frankly clueless about the businesses they were in; sales professionals who actually had no significant sales skills and even less dedication to either that craft or to effectively serving clients . . . they all found themselves rolling in easy money. This has happened a number of times before. When times are good, the CEO looks like a genius and the sales reps look like superstars. But when the first rough waters come along, these same people suddenly look like bumbling idiots.

Have they actually changed that much? No—they were never very sharp in the first place. And their blaming of everything on the economy is a giant, destructive lie. Denial and delusion. When the economy as a whole or isolated within a particular industry, field, or geographic area turns from overly generous and agreeable to miserly and grumpy, weakness, vulnerabilities, laziness, poor discipline, and shallow know-how is all exposed. The Wall Street expression is: you can't see who's naked . . . or be certain who is "inadequate" . . . until the tide goes *out*.

The blunt truth is this: if you insist on blaming anything but yourself for unsatisfactory results, you can't exercise enough control to get satisfactory results. If you're going to achieve high levels of success in selling, you've got to be able to produce positive results in any and all circumstances including those viewed by most as negative circumstances. You have to choose and decide, which kind of sales professional you are going to be: a fair weather salesperson or an all-weather salesperson.

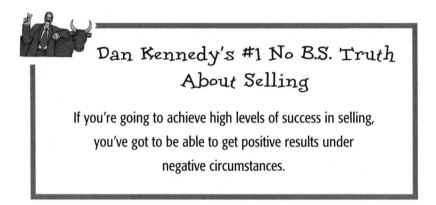

Dan Kennedy's #1 No B.S. Truth About Selling

If you're going to achieve high levels of success in selling, you've got to be able to get positive results under negative circumstances.

Anyway, back to the war story. I made up my mind that I had to sell these angry, neglected customers on keeping our line in their stores and even buying more. I had to get positive results under these very negative circumstances. I had to face customers who had been lied to, inconvenienced, billed for merchandise they couldn't sell, dunned for payment, and otherwise abused, and somehow get them to "forgive and forget." In order to do this, *I had to take my ego out of the way.*

In different selling situations, different things get in the way. You can never actually remove those placed in your way

by others—be they the boneheads in Washington running the economy, a tough competitor, or in this case, my own company's management that permitted this awful situation to develop. But you can remove whatever obstacles you place in your own way. Those are almost always reactions to circumstances, and those are entirely within your control. Make a note.

Anyway, through all the work I've done training salespeople and working with sales executives struggling to get productivity from salespeople, I've discovered that the number one secret reason for failure in selling is ego. The person with an inflated ego or with very fragile self-esteem (the two are connected) *perceives refusal as rejection.* When someone says no to such a person, he or she takes it personally.

Confusing refusal with rejection makes selling painful, because more people say no than ever say yes. In a difficult economy, this can be truer; a "worse" ratio, as resistance to spending anything on anything sets in. In the emerging New Economy, that newly learned resistance will linger longer after actual recession has departed, just as it did for survivors of the first Great Depression. And, in The New Economy, customers will demand clearer, better, more "on target" value propositions, so there will be more rejection, at least en-route to the eventual sale. In my situation, of course, they were well beyond simple refusal to buy. Customers were calling me vile names, throwing things at me. I had to remember that it really had nothing to do with me. These people weren't mad at me; they were mad at the previous rep, at the company, or at the situation—but not at me.

I've since learned that just about any time an individual disagrees with me, fails to accept an offer I present, says no to me, or otherwise interferes with my access to what I want, it very rarely has anything to do with me as a person, And since it isn't personal, it doesn't warrant any kind of an emotional reaction. Having control over your emotions gives you a very powerful advantage in selling.

As I approached these hostile customers, I took my emotions out of the situation. No matter what they said, I interpreted it as reasonable, justifiable anger at other people and at a negative situation. I listened. I was patient. I was concerned. And I never got angry. I never got defensive. Finally, when the customer had vented and had nothing more to say, I asked for permission to respond. I stated the obvious: I had no control over the past. I could only exercise control over the present. My job now was to make handling the merchandise so profitable and pleasurable for the merchant that it made up for all the past problems and justified a renewed relationship. Then I shifted right into selling—just as if the customer was new and had never heard of the company, the books, or me. I've since learned, by the way, that in every situation, there is a point when the opportunity to shift into selling presents itself.

It worked. But even while it was working, many of the customers questioned my integrity. They wanted to know whether or not I was telling the truth. They asked whether I would keep my promises concerning service. They were skeptical and suspicious. If I had wanted to be thin-skinned, I could have gotten angry with them. How dare they question *my* honesty?

Again, I had to understand that this, too, was nothing personal. I chose to work for a company that had "done them wrong" once. I had to accept the consequences, including guilt by association. Again, I had to set my ego aside.

With this approach, I saved twice as many accounts as I lost. I even returned to that first drugstore and got the merchandise back in. I had discovered that initial refusal, even antagonism, was not necessarily the ultimate result. I discovered that I could change a no to a yes more often than not.

My favorite illustration of all this comes from my first call on the head buyer for the book departments of a major department store chain. I went with one of the company's experienced salespeople, as an apprentice, to watch and learn. I was to carry the samples and keep my mouth shut.

Keeping quiet was no problem; I sat in stunned silence as the other sales rep presented the buyer with one new title after another. As he looked at each book, the buyer kept saying: "This is crap. Do you know that? Why should I have this crap in my store? How can you show me this crap?" The buyer went on and on like that, and the sales rep did not say a word! Finally, the buyer picked up one sample after the other and barked: "Ship me ten dozen" or "Ship me 50." This went on for nearly an hour and the sales rep rarely spoke. The buyer criticized and cussed each sample, then ordered. When it was over, the rep had written an order for close to $10,000.00—a very, very big order in that business. He and the buyer shook hands, exchanged pleasantries, and we left. I couldn't believe what I had witnessed.

The sales rep said, "You know, he always does that. The first few times I went in there, years ago, I got mad at him. I got defensive. I argued with him. Finally he took pity on me. He asked me a great question: What do you care what I think of this stuff or say about this stuff as long as I buy a lot of it and my stores sell a lot of it and you make a lot of money?"

I have been a very serious student of Dr. Maxwell Maltz' work since I was in my teens. Dr. Maltz' best known book, *Psycho-Cybernetics*, has sold over 30 million copies worldwide. His works have had such important impact on me, several years ago I acquired all the rights to all his works, co-authored new ones, including *The New Psycho-Cybernetics* book. One of the key things I learned from "Psycho-Cybernetics" was how to develop a strong self-image bulletproof against all unimportant criticism. I have also long been a very serious student of first-generation millionaires and multi-millionaires who've gotten there by building businesses from scratch. I've had hundreds of these people as clients and associates, and developed my *Renegade Millionaire System* (www.RenegadeMillionaire.com) based on them. A commonality key in the majority: strong immunity to criticism. This is a theme you'll find running through the top performers in selling as well. **They care little about what people *think*; they care about what people *buy*.**

No's Turned into Yes's,
That's What Master Salespeople Do

For ten years, concluded at my choice, I had the great privilege of touring North America, appearing as a speaker on the same seminar programs with legendary sales and success speaker Zig Ziglar, as well as Brian Tracy, Jim Rohn, Tom Hopkins, and numerous celebrities, addressing audiences of thousands to as many as 35,000 in each city. Zig is one of the "masters" I studied at the very beginning of my selling life. One of his stories, that stuck in my mind permanently features the sales woman who couldn't hear a "no" shouted in her ear, but could hear a whispered "yes" from 50 paces. For years that was the right approach: simply ignoring the word "no." In The New Economy, that's too simplistic. You now need some sensitivity to the reasons, the secret reasons, the psychology behind people saying "no," so you can design sales presentations that acknowledge but pre-empt them. *Then* you can be deaf to them and sell past them.

People start out by saying "no" to things for many, many reasons. For some, it's an automatic, knee-jerk, defense mechanism. They may not fully understand the matter you are dealing with, and be too embarrassed to admit it. They may not know how to intelligently make a decision. They may lack self-confidence and self-esteem. They may be afraid. They may have financial problems that (in their minds) preclude them from going along with you. There are hundreds of possible reasons for "the erroneous no." Don't let it stop you.

As the recession deepened, new emotional reasons for particularly affluent clients saying no developed, which you'll find discussed in the article reprinted from *The No B.S. Marketing to the Affluent Letter* immediately following the end of this chapter. At the time you read this, these reasons for saying no (even when they want to say yes) may or may not still be prevalent among affluent customers—I can't predict. But regardless, they serve as a fine illustration that there are more impractical reasons than practical ones for saying no, that reasons for saying no are always changing but some are always there, and every such impediment can be countered if approached thoughtfully, and if you refuse to accept it as governing reality.

I believe sales professionals will hear "no" more often from more customers in The New Economy. These no's will signal many different obstacles to the sale that need addressed. They must be heard with no emotional response to them, they must be addressed in a way meaningful to the customer, and, ultimately, they must be ignored and not permitted to end the selling process.

Eight Steps for Getting Past No

1. Determine that you are going to exert control over the situation and the other people involved.
2. Determine that you can and will get positive results even in negative situations.
3. Get your ego out of the way.
4. Do not confuse refusal with rejection.
5. Be more interested in achieving positive results than in anything else.
6. Understand that most no's are erroneous.
7. Ignore the "erroneous no." Keep making your case. Keep probing for the real reason for reluctance or refusal. **Acknowledge but never accept**.
8. Respond only to real reasons. Don't get caught up in responding to "erroneous no's"—that's like wrestling with a phantom.

Understanding, remembering, and using these eight steps will help you convert many refusals to ultimate acceptance.

However, having said all this, a much, much smarter approach is to place yourself in Low-Resistance Selling Situations, where these techniques aren't as important. A great deal of traditional sales training focuses on "closing" but I maintain, if you need to "close", you opened poorly; the close should be effortless, painless, automatic. As you'll discover, the vast majority of this book is devoted to helping you engineer Low-Resistance Selling Situations rather than succeeding in tough sales situations.

Still, having said that, the size of your income in selling will be representative of the strength of your emotional immunity to the word "no."

The New Realities of the Affluent

It has been about a year since my NO B.S. MARKETING TO THE AFFLUENT book was first published, and it was written, sealed, and delivered to its publisher about 6 months before that. Obviously, much has changed since then. I predicted and allowed for most of it, although the depth and extent of the destruction has surprised even me, and the combined ignorance, stupidity, and arrogance of those now in charge who are worsening the trouble with their every meddling is greater than even I imagined. Still, in re-reading my own book this week, I find most of it perfectly applicable, some of it particularly relevant. Chapter 16, for example, now has double purpose; it talks about selling "little indulgences" to mass affluents who trade up, but is now just as useful in marketing to wounded affluents foregoing major luxuries and more desirous of little ones, as salve for wounds.

Here is more about the new realities . . .

By most accounts, the affluent have done very well: those in the top 10% of incomes have seen their incomes rise 34% after inflation since 1979 (while those in the bottom 10% have seen a paltry 4% increase—although there's no correlation). It is the gains of the rich that have spawned massive growth in luxury housing, real estate, countless consumer services—from maid and housecleaning services to lawn care to pet-sitting, and invention of new businesses like fractional jet ownership. The spending of the affluent has been and is a considerable economic driver. 1.2-million luxury cars were sold in '08, for example; about 15% of total, net U.S. auto sales, but a much higher contribution to profit. This "power spending class" is now reigning itself in, in varying degrees, in different product and service categories—another problem for the economy as a whole, and a new advertising, marketing, and sales challenge for those who rely on them. For the economy, luxury-industry unemployment is at 15%+, in retail, in home building, in top-upscale restaurants. For the marketers, creating new value propositions has been key: Ritz-Carlton, Bergdorfs, and their peer companies are all aggressive in "bundling", packaging and discounting. In Vail, Colorado, luxury ski resort operators report a slump in occupancy over previous years, which they are attacking, with some success, by getting more last-minute customers, lured with overt direct offers, featuring extra free days, free meals, meal plans and discounts.

Affluent hesitancy to spend at this time revolves around three things: one, actual, diminished capacity or *anticipated* diminished capacity; two, being more selective and demanding about value for dollars spent i.e., spending decisions less casual; and three, concern about inappropriateness of high-end spending. The General Manager of a dealership selling Bentley, Rolls-Royce, and Lotus says his customers can still afford to indulge but express to him the thought that showing up in a new luxury car when friends or colleagues are losing their jobs or businesses may seem de-classe. To this last point, just throwing your money around or flaunting your spending is "so pre-recession." Shoppers at high-end boutiques are asking for plain bags or home delivery; a Gucci store reports delivering a $1,200.00 bag wrapped as a gift so no one would know the person bought it for herself. The owner of a New Jersey manufacturing company told a reporter he was unaffected, was proceeding with his annual family vacation to the Bahamas, but "trying to be more covert." Barbara Lazaroff, Wolfgang Puck's ex-wife and business partner, says their upscale restaurants are still busy, but customers skip the $300.00 bottles of wine—"they want to *seem respectful of the recession."* Making it acceptable to spend is an interesting challenge. It suggests more non-profit and charity tie-ins; tying practical arguments to desires for a purchase, making it more rationally defensible; using the recession and the unusual savings opportunities to forces as good, sensible reason to buy now. Senseless extravagant spending is out; but *sensible* extravagant spending is alive and well.

At its core, this is all nothing more—or less—than my Message-Market Match. Kraft is hurrying ten new DiGiorgio pizzas to market in recession response, promoted as just like pizza delivered from Pizza Hut, etc., but at half the price . . . and new flavors of Kool-Aid, advertised as "more smiles per gallon," less costly than soda pop. Right for *their* market. If selling to the affluent, and selling premium-priced goods or services, obviously a different message has always been required; now it has to incorporate additional elements that address the above three issues. More complex marketing messages, more care, more thought, better targeting.

(*Sources*: Associated Press wire service article, "The Wealthy Turn Stealthy," 1-27-09. Sent in by Luxury Member Jan Duke, the Glazer-Kennedy Independent Business Advisor in Chico/Redding, California; and *USA TODAY* 2-2-09)

This article is reprinted from *The No B.S. Marketing to the Affluent Letter*, one of a family of business, marketing, and sales newsletters and other resources published by Glazer-Kennedy Insider's Circle LLC. For information about these publications, a free trial offer, free introductory webinars, and other resources, visit www.FreeGiftFrom.com.sales.

CHAPTER 2

STRATEGY 2
THE POSITIVE POWER OF
NEGATIVE PREPARATION

I've been involved in what I've labeled "the success education business" since 1976. For decades, I was an active member of the National Speakers Association—fraternizing and consulting with hundreds of people who earn their livings as professional lecturers and seminar leaders, including some whose names you know. I helped create the Information Marketing Association, the more encompassing trade-professional association inclusive of speakers, trainers, coaches, consultants, authors, and publishers (www.info-marketing.org). Throughout these years, I've spoken to nearly 7,000,000 people from the platform, maybe more, about success-oriented topics. I've delivered as many as 100 "live" speaking presentations a year, for major corporations, associations, and at large public events, plus countless teleseminars and webinars, and only in the last couple of years have I deliberately cut back that pace.

For that purpose, for my own use, and for the many speakers and information marketers I've had as clients, I've become exceptionally adept at and very well-known for structuring and writing "platform sales presentations"—sort of a combination of speech writing and sales presentation or script development. I've been paid upwards from $100,000.00 to craft such presentations. I have also been highly paid to create sales presentations delivered via television infomercials, complex direct-mail packages incorporating "long form" sales letters from 16 to 64 pages in length, and via other media. It has all made me a proponent of "negative preparation."

I have frequently been mislabeled and misintroduced as a "motivational speaker," from the platform, in meetings, at cocktail parties. As a result, I've had more conversations than I care to count with my students, clients, customers, peers, and friends about "positive thinking." Through it all, I've come to the conclusion that *at least 95% of the people who think they're positive thinkers actually have no idea what positive thinking is really all about.*

Too many people think it's some kind of mystical, magical shield from the real world. They believe that if they just think positive, bad things cannot happen to them. If something bad happens to somebody, they say: "See, you weren't thinking positively." But it just doesn't work that way. You can think positive until you are turning blue from the effort, but you'll still run into obstacles from time to time. People who believe that positive thinking is supposed to keep the bogeyman away eventually wind up frustrated, discouraged critics of positive thinking.

Being a positive thinker does *not* mean that you should refuse to acknowledge the way things are. In fact, people succeed in business, sales, and marketing by dealing with "what is" not with "what ought to be." **The true positive thinker acknowledges potential and existing negative circumstances and reactions,** and engineers a plan to overcome them, to achieve positive results. In selling or negotiating, I call this *the positive power of negative preparation.*

How General Patton Used the Positive Power of Negative Preparation

There's a great sequence in the movie *Patton* where General Patton is dozing the night before a battle. He has a book in his lap: Field Marshal Rommel's book on tactics. The next day Patton's troops drive Rommel's troops off the battlefield into retreat. As the gunfire and other noise ends, Patton is standing alone, leaning forward, stage whispering across the battlefield:

"Rommel—I read your book."

Some people would say that acknowledging Rommel's expertise as a tactician and preparing to counter any possible successful moves was being negative. They're wrong. It was positively brilliant.

In several of the most successful, profitable, complex negotiations I've been involved in—buying and selling businesses, assembling capital, developing relationships with celebrities, manufacturers, and producers in the TV infomercial business— I've prepared by anticipating and writing down every possible question, concern, and objection the other party could raise, and then formulating my responses in advance. I carefully analyzed every weakness in my position that might be attacked and thought of ways to respond effectively. I thought of every possible thing that could screw up the deal and then thought of some preventive measure to take in each case. I was thoroughly prepared, *from a negative perspective.*

WARNING: If your prime selling years have been the 1980s into the mid 2000s, you've been selling to relatively *noncritical customers.* Their incomes and net worth were increasing, in many cases, multiplying; real estate values and other investments' values all steadily escalating or, in some cases, leaping in big bounds; credit was cheap and plentiful; and there was a heady mix of aspiration, ambition, and unbridled optimism, sometimes called "irrational exuberance," in the air. Customers entered the buying environment and the activity of buying predisposed to buy, and absent tendency to be skeptical or critical. If you think you've *been* overcoming buying resistance, you ain't seen nothin' yet! What felt like gale force wind to you, given no frame of reference from selling during prior, serious recessions, wasn't even a stiff breeze.

Now, in the post-recession, emerging New Economy, you will be selling to customers conditioned to be critical. To be critical thinkers about value, quality, service after the sale, comparable alternatives, and more. Other good words to describe these New Economy Customers are: cautious, circumspect, guarded, discerning, judicial. And one of the most cautionary synonyms of "critical" is: fault-finding. To work successfully with these New Economy Customers, it is more vital than ever to thoroughly prepare, from a negative perspective.

One of the times I sold one of my companies—that entire process, from first approaching my chosen buyer to cashing the check took only 6 days. In another instance, I sold another of my businesses in fewer than 20 days. These are typically complex sales situations fraught with peril, from deal-killing lawyers to hidden agendas to misunderstandings, and on and on. The speed with which I completed these sales is testament in large part to careful negative preparation. Business-to-business sales professionals often ask about strategies for abbreviating normally long sales cycles, and this is one of the best: negative preparation, disclosure and resolution early and all at once, rather than hoping the buyer does not think of "x," and subsequently having negatives drip out, trickle out, to be handled one by one.

Who Else Uses the Positive Power of Negative Preparation?

I'm a bit of a sports freak, and as a speaker, I've had the terrific opportunity of spending time backstage in 'the green room' with champion athletes like Troy Aikman, Joe Montana, Peyton Manning, George Foreman, and with top coaches including the late Tom Landry, Lou Holtz, and Jimmy Johnson. My friends in the world of sports have included Brendan Suhr, who has been an assistant head coach of three NBA teams. Another is Bill Foster, former head basketball coach at Northwestern University and one of the "winningest" coaches in college basketball history.

I have talked about this subject with all of them, and found consensus. These champions have super-strength positive attitudes, but they also wisely use the positive power of negative preparation.

Most successful coaches go into each game with more than one prepared game plan. They have a plan to follow if their team gets ahead early in the game. They have a different plan to follow if their team falls behind. They have alternate plans ready to use different combinations of players in case one key player is injured during the game. That's not negative thinking; that's the positive power of negative preparation at work.

As I said at the top of this chapter, I've done a lot of work in planning, scripting, and implementing group sales presentations, and training others to do the same. What I call "group presentation marketing" applies to everything from a Tupperware party to a seminar designed to sell $50,000.00 real estate partnerships. There are a lot of special techniques for this type of selling, but one of the most important is the anticipation and removal of the reasons for refusal or procrastination on the audience's part. Sometimes this is done with subtlety, weaving the objections and responses into the presentation. Other times it's done quite openly. One very successful presentation I designed ended with the presenter listing the four main reasons why people don't join—and then answering every one of them.

You also have to do this when you are selling in print. I am paid from a low of $50,000.00 to $150,000.00 plus royalties as a direct-response copywriter, to write full page newspaper and magazine ads, sales letters, infomercials, and other marketing documents, and over 85% of all clients who use me once do so repeatedly—despite my fees. Why? One reason is my very thorough negative preparation. When I'm creating an advertisement, brochure, or direct-mail piece, I make a list of every reason I can think of why the reader would *not* respond to the offer. I use that list of "negatives" as a guide in writing the copy. This approach produces some of the most powerful selling in print in the world.

If this strategy is important to us, the people behind the scenes, who get paid as much to write one sales letter as many professionals earn in six months, then it is important to you, too!

Six Steps for Using the Positive Power of Negative Preparation

1. Forget preconceived labels of "positive" or negative."
2. Make a list of every question, concern, or objection that the other person could possibly come up with.
3. Make a list of everything that could go wrong.
4. Develop positive responses to all the negatives you've thought of.
5. Have your information, ideas, and documentation well organized so that you can lay your hands on the appropriate notes and materials at a moment's notice.
6. Take great confidence from your thorough preparation.

CHAPTER 3

STRATEGY 3
USE LISTENING TO INFLUENCE PEOPLE

H ere's my super-powerful secret selling weapon: I listen.

Listening isn't as simple as it sounds. In fact, the absence of good listening skills is rated as one of the top problems in North American business today. On the job accidents, manufacturing errors, medicine dispensing mistakes in hospitals…the list of costs, financial and human, attributed to listening errors is long. Some major corporations invest huge sums of money in listening skills training for their personnel. My biggest complaint with people I work with is their lack of listening effectiveness; I explain something deliberately and precisely, but they get only part of what I'm saying. So, the first problem is that most people lack know-how in listening. For the sales professional, this is double jeopardy: his own listening deficiencies, and those of his customers.

The second problem is even those who CAN listen often DON'T, for all the following and many other reasons:

Preoccupied with Other Thoughts

If you could see what was going on in the other person's mind, like images on a TV screen, you'd be shocked. Something related to what you are saying might appear every once in a while, but there'd be a rush of other, unrelated images in between.

When I'm speaking to an audience, I know that a fast-paced parade of images is going through their heads: a kitchen on fire—"Gee, I wonder if I turned off the coffee pot?"; the super-market—"What should I make for dinner?"; an angry spouse slamming the door—"She's so unreasonable"; and on and on. They leave me and my presentation, mentally, then come back, leave again, and come back. In fact, psychologists say people mentally leave every four to eight minutes for sexual fantasy. The good news is, I know everybody in the audience'll have a good time regardless of what I do. The bad news is, I'm up there to sell, and need their attention. I *know* they're leaving; I must pull them back in. It is a huge face-to-face selling mistake to assume you have the other person's attention just because he's looking at you.

Adult attention deficit disorder has been multiplied by technology. These days, most people are continuously connected to multiple stimuli. Nobody seems able to just take a walk; they require music from headphones *and* text messaging at the same time. Television news has type scrolling across the bottom of the screen, split-screen images, and more graphics going on around the talking head than you can find in a comic book. It is against this backdrop that we try to get and hold someone's attention while we sell to them. Their actual ability to pay attention is lessened with each new wave of multistimuli connectivity they plug into. And your actual ability to pay attention has been lessened too. Simply, purely, completely concentrating on what your customer is saying is counter to all the ongoing behavioral conditioning you're exposed to and all the other experiences you're involved in. Getting your customer to concentrate on what you are saying requires behavior from him that is contrary to all the on-going conditioning he's exposed to.

The sales pro has to master methods for disconnecting all those other thoughts and ignoring all other stimuli and distractions and focusing entirely and exclusively on the prospect or client . . . before he can hope to get that customer to do so in return.

Tired

I'm guilty of this myself. After a few days of traveling, speaking, and consulting, a level of fatigue sets in that just about ruins my ability to listen.

It's worth noting that being properly rested and alert is an advantage in selling or negotiating. The sales pro who stays up too late night after night, or who schedules important meetings too close together, or employs an excessively exhausting travel schedule starts each selling situation with a handicap. Personally, I find both travel and selling activity require incredible physical energy. Avoiding fatigue-inducing foods, sticking to a healthy diet as best I can, seeing my chiropractor and massage therapist regularly, and taking carefully selected nutritional supplements are all lifestyle techniques I believe give me an edge in my selling activities.

In Too Much of a Hurry

It is easy and dangerous to be consumed by speed rather than to profit from efficiency. These days, it seems the sales pro never gets a breather; he lets his cell phone, e-mail, text messaging, etc.

control him; he tries to run marathons as sprints. The trick is to use speed to your advantage and to prevent it from becoming a disadvantage. If you have a tendency, as I do, to get caught up in the pace of things going on around you, and to build up stress in the process, it's important to consciously s-l-o-w y-o-u-r-s-e-l-f d-o-w-n in most selling situations. Listening effectively cannot be done at warp speed. You have to disengage from the race pace and shift into a relaxed selling pace. Another way of saying this is: let the sale come to you.

Operating in Disadvantageous Conditions and Environments

With mobile communications technology tools comes the temptation to completely confuse urgent and important, and be stampeded into responding to inquiries by prospects and customers thoughtlessly, even recklessly, on the spur of the moment, and in unhelpful environments—noisy restaurants or airport terminals, moving vehicles in heavy traffic, or while multitasking, such as driving and navigating through heavy traffic, or even standing at a urinal in a public restroom, peeing. (Yes, ladies, idiot men in large numbers are making this commonplace behavior. What you hear in the background while they're talking to you isn't a fountain.)

LISTEN TO ME: environment matters. If you wouldn't sit down face to face with somebody and attempt selling to them in a given environment because it is chaotic, full of disruptions, or otherwise not conducive to concentrating, listening, and communicating effectively, don't sell from there by phone either. It's stupid. Also, communicating about important matters to important people via thoughtlessly and hastily used means; instant response via an e-mail tapped out on your iPhone while eating, standing in a waiting area at the airport, or, God forbid, sitting on the toilet is also s-t-u-p-i-d. If you engage in this kind of moronic and unprofessional and sloppy, slap-dash behavior,

"Can you hang on a sec? I think I just took another picture of my ear."

know that I am hoping and praying for your failure. This is no way to conduct *business*.

As a result of all this, nobody's listening to anybody. And since people generally want most what they have the least of, many are running around in desperate search of someone—*anyone*—who will make them feel important by listening to what they have to say. There is enormous opportunity in knowing and understanding that.

My friend Sydney Barrows, author of the excellent book *Uncensored Sales Strategies* was, in her former life, in distant past, a professional madam, and ultimately an infamous one, dubbed The Mayflower Madam, first by New York media, then nationally. For a time, she operated the priciest upscale escort service in New York, hiring, training, and dispatching elegant young ladies to entertain corporate executives, Wall Street elite, visiting foreign dignitaries, as well as thousands of more run-of-the-mill businessmen and "road warriors" alone at night in the city's hotel rooms. While it is not all about that, her book does give you an insider's look at many of that business' secrets and the sales and marketing lessons to be drawn from it. From that experience, Sydney learned and can assure you they were never in anything as crass or simple as the business of selling sex. And one of the most important things they did sell, in high demand, was an intelligent, fully focused, interested, and appreciative *listener*. The fact that even highly successful and influential men find reason to pay hundreds of thousands of dollars an hour to be listened to—by therapist in a professional practice or lady of the evening in hotel suite—should tell you something significant.

This is "as old as the hills" but it has not changed. Neither psychotherapy or prostitution including pricey escort services is leaving our world anytime soon. In fact, the desperate desire to

Uncensored Sales Strategies

Visit: www.EntrepreneurPress.com/UncensoredSales.html for information about Sydney Barrows' uncensored sales strategies—for mature sales professionals only! Pick up the book, *Uncensored Sales Strategies* at any fine bookseller. This book presents a radical new approach to selling your customers what they really want, no matter what business you're in!

be listened to, and willingness to reward it financially, are both expanding and escalating. Recently, a friend of mine, a business-woman in her 40s, expressed her frustration to me with this story:

> "I was asked to join another business woman, a friend of the past I'd been out of touch with for a while for lunch. In the first 15 minutes we were together, she took calls, returned a call, and talked on her cell phone incessantly— and sent a text message. I got up to visit the ladies room and told her 'If you're still making out with that damned phone when I come back, I see no reason to stay and watch.'"

If this businesswoman who invited my friend to lunch had ulterior motives of laying groundwork for selling her something, which she most certainly did, she ruined it with her rudeness. Of course, you might never be so overtly rude or stupid. But if the phone is locked away, but your mind is visiting it, the effect is the same.

By training and disciplining myself to listen—really listen— I've been able to exert tremendous influence over many other people. I've gained their trust, stimulated friendship, gotten them to confide in me, and sold to them with ease. I've discovered that you *can* exchange attention for dollars! I'm now convinced that the person who gets his or her own way most often is the person doing a lot more listening than talking.

What Are You Listening *For*?

In selling, you should be listening *with purpose*. Not just to build rapport, not to be polite, not to flatter, not to seduce, but more for strategic acquisition of important and useful information. I've labeled this "Listening-Based Selling," and taught it to thousands of salespeople. In doing so, I discovered a crying need for a "tool" to support their Listening-Based Selling.

If you don't know what you hope to hear, you might not recognize it when you do hear it. I've compiled a checklist of 21 things to listen for, which you can download free at NoBSBooks.com. For now, here are several of the most important:

1. *What keeps him up at night unable to sleep, bile crawling up his esophagus from frustration, anger, and resentment?* (Note: Relief of pain sells more than potential gain.)
2. *What does he fear and worry about most?* (Note: Fear is the most powerful of all motivational forces.)
3. *What overriding value is most important to him,* as demonstrated by his behavior and prioritized actions, not just lip service—is it "family," "marriage," "career achievement," "wealth," "security," what?

There are 18 others. My 21 may or may not all apply to your particular selling situations so, ultimately, you should construct and memorize your own checklist. Then you'll listen with purpose. And you'll be able to quantify and measure your listening effectiveness. After a first conversation with a client, I measure mine by how many of the 21 things I was listening for I heard and remember. Since measurement automatically improves performance, you'll become a much more effective listener with this discipline.

To be redundant to be clear, I have just handed you two very specific things to do. Not "ideas." Things to do, to measurably strengthen the listening part of your selling game. 1): Develop a list of what you are listening for. In writing. 2): After every meeting or conversation, but especially after initial meetings or conversations, grade yourself by how many of the items on your list you acquired information, insight, and understanding about.

Would you care to guess what percentage of sales professionals reading this book will actually put together that tool and engage in that scoring?

How to Read Anyone's Mind

Early in my business life, I traveled to New York, to a private meeting at the palatial office of the CEO of a large, fast-growing public company. I was being considered for a very important, very big, very lucrative consulting assignment, potentially worth hundreds of thousands of dollars to me. In the 40 minutes or so of this meeting, we actually dealt with the matter at hand for only 10 minutes, and I listened, for half of those minutes. For the other half hour, I mostly listened to the CEO talk about his problems of the day, expound on his business philosophy, brag about his most recent big deal, and unintentionally tell me exactly what he wanted to hear from me to make our deal. I sat there and quietly "read his mind."

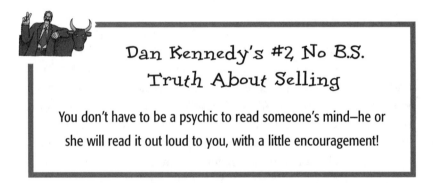

Dan Kennedy's #2, No B.S. Truth About Selling

You don't have to be a psychic to read someone's mind—he or she will read it out loud to you, with a little encouragement!

Way back in 1993, I wrote a small book about this subject: HOW TO READ ANYONE'S MIND. It has been out of print for years, but now you have it, as a Bonus Book, at the end of this one. I have added only a few updated references, but largely preserved the original text as-is.

Five Steps to Listening More Effectively

1. *Clear your mind of distractions before getting into a meeting with another person or other people.* Take a minute to close

your eyes and blank your mind immediately before going into a meeting or picking up the telephone. Top telemarketing trainers tell people handling incoming calls to set aside their paperwork on the first ring, close their eyes, and take a deep breath on the second ring, then smile and answer on the third ring.

2. *Determine in advance why the person you are going to be listening to is important to you, and why what he or she is saying might be important to you.* You have to sell yourself on the relevance in order to focus your attention.

3. *Listen for information and insight that you can use to engineer cooperation with the other person.* A long, apparently irrelevant, favorite story told by the other person may inadvertently reveal one tiny clue to effectively persuading or motivating that person.

4. *Be an active listener.* Nod. Give feedback. Ask questions to encourage the person to continue and to demonstrate your interest. Use the technique of "mirroring"* to put the other person at ease. This is not to advise sacrificing personality and individuality. I certainly haven't and I don't believe anybody else should. But you can keep your individuality and still modify your physiology, within a range, to make the person you are listening to feel more comfortable.

5. *In some business situations, it may be appropriate to jot down notes as you listen.* Don't hesitate to do so; it helps illustrate your interest.

---

*"Mirroring" is an NLP (Neuro-Linguistic Programming) term. Many sales professionals, speakers, and negotiators study and employ NLP techniques.

CHAPTER 4

STRATEGY 4
AVOID CONTAMINATION

I n just about every sales organization lurk "grizzled veterans" who, through a combination of longevity, seniority, and accumulated customers or clients, manage to earn reasonably good livings even though they are poor salespeople. These hangers-on make money in spite of their many bad habits. *These people are extremely dangerous to any enthusiastic salesperson,* but especially to any new salesperson for a number of reasons:

- *They are not fully aware* of all their own counter-productive attitudes and habits, and they are capable of unintentionally contaminating others.
- *They resent hotshots* who might make them look lazy, ineffective, or over-the-hill and will consciously and subconsciously do things to put the over-achiever in his place.

The person who actively aspires to top performance, who displays initiative, drive, and determination, or who challenges the status quo with new and different ways of doing things is their enemy—and they will do whatever they can to directly discourage him and, behind his back, undermine him.

- *They do not keep up-to-date and informed* on the latest sales techniques and product information, so they are likely to be sources of outdated or inaccurate information even though they sound authoritative and knowledgeable.

- *They often have very poor personal habits*, including drinking at lunch and after work on a daily basis, using foul language, and sometimes even poor personal hygiene.

- *They are cynical about people.* They often call customers or clients "marks," "pigeons," and other derogatory names. *You cannot succeed in selling in a big way if you are cynical about people or about your clientele.* (Note that it's okay to be realistic, just not cynical; there is a difference.)

- *They are complainers and blamers*—that's how they excuse their own mediocrity. In order to succeed in selling, you must take full responsibility for every factor in the process. These people are particularly hazardous during difficult economic times, during times of upheaval or change, or during emergence of this or any subsequent New Economy, because they view and talk about all change as adversity and obstacle—never as opportunity.

Every business, every company, every organization has at least a few of these types. You will find them on the showroom floor at the car dealership, gathered around the coffee machine in the real estate office, in the hall, or at the sales meeting. You must not let these people contaminate you! They are *toxic*.

Very recently, I worked with a client stuck with three veteran salespeople stubbornly unwilling to make outbound telephone calls generated by the advertising I'd developed. They insisted these were poor quality leads, "mooches" as they put it, who had requested free information and product samples from the ads but had no real interest in the high-priced product being sold. At my urging, he hired three new, additional salespeople just to follow up on these leads—but he put them in the same office as the first two. In less than two weeks, the old veterans ruined the new ones. The new reps had a brief, initial flurry of success, then their results diminished. Later, we again got three new salespeople installed and safely isolated in a distant building, and they produced millions of dollars of business from those "mooches." Old dogs who refuse to learn new tricks should never be permitted to raise puppies.

How to Cheat on Your Expense Account and Other "Lessons" from the Grizzled Old Pro

Early in my selling career, a manager flew in to work with me in my territory. He and I traveled together for a week. He taught me several creative ways to cheat on my expense account and how to make sales calls by phone and write them up as if they were made in person. He taught me virtually nothing about selling. He was a great "pal." He had a terrific if slightly bizarre sense of humor, and he was making reasonably good money. But he had nothing to offer that would help me achieve my goals.

Shortly after being hired, I went to Chicago to work the company's exhibit booth in the Chicago Gift Show. This is a huge trade show, where tens of thousands of gift shop owners and chain store buyers come in search of new, different, and sellable merchandise. I was excited about being there and eager to write a lot of business with the people attending from my territory. Almost instantly the other sales pros ganged up on me, saying things like, "Take it easy—we're gonna be here for four long days"; "Don't be too aggressive—it looks bad"; "Most of these

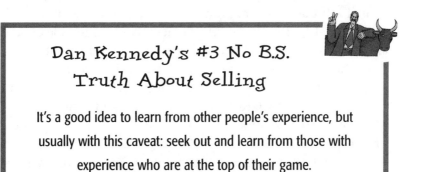
people are just lookers, not buyers, anyway"; "Nobody sells much at these shows—we're here to get leads."

I ignored the whole bunch of them and, much to their irritation, wrote thousands of dollars of orders during the show. No huge amount—nothing to write home about—but it was more than what five of the others (who had at least six years' more experience than I did) made.

Those experiences taught me that it was generally unwise to listen to advice, complaints, and comments of others just because they were older or more experienced. Age is not necessarily equivalent to wisdom. Experience does not always teach much. In fact, since most people stop learning very early in their careers, you are very likely to encounter the person who has one year's experience 30 times rather than 30 years of experience.

Dan Kennedy's #3 No B.S. Truth About Selling

It's a good idea to learn from other people's experience, but usually with this caveat: seek out and learn from those with experience who are at the top of their game.

You must exercise great care in selecting those who are permitted to advise and influence you. Falling under the influence of someone headed nowhere will generally lead you to the same destination!

These toxic associations must be avoided at all costs. On the other hand, association with success-minded, progressive individuals engaged in improving their knowledge and skills in sales, marketing, and other business disciplines is well worth the search to find it or effort invested in creating it. Along these lines, I have a "commercial" recommendation: I'm pleased to tell you that we have local Glazer-Kennedy Insider's Circle™ Chapters meeting regularly in over 150 towns and cities throughout the United States and Canada, as well as Dan Kennedy Study/ Mastermind Groups in most of those areas. They are facilitated by trained, certified, and very capable Independent Business Advisors, and the local entrepreneurs, business owners, self-employed professionals, and sales professionals participating are people you will benefit from hanging out with. For information and, in most areas, a free guest pass to attend a Chapter meeting, visit the Directory of Certified No B.S. Business Advisors and Chapters at www.DanKennedy.com.

There is probably no profession other than selling where mental attitude is as important, with the possible sharing with professional sports. The late W. Clement Stone, self-made billionaire, who began as a star insurance sales pro and taught tens of thousands of others how to excel in that field while building the largest independent insurance sales organization of its time, out of the depths of the Great Depression, summed it up this way: "The sale is contingent on the attitude of the salesperson, not the prospect." It is for that reason that you must militantly protect your mental attitude from contamination. Your success will be contingent on your mental attitude, not the attitude of your customers or clients.

Oh, and incidentally, Stone didn't say "The sale is contingent upon the attitude of the salesperson, not the prospect—unless times are tough, unless there's recession, unless there's a tough competitor in the game, unless . . . ." No weasel words, no escape clause here.

CHAPTER 5

STRATEGY 5
THE PROCESS OF
PERSONAL PACKAGING

I have a lot of experience in the advertising business, so I often think in terms of advertising. One big factor in the advertising and marketing of most products is *packaging*. Different packaging is appropriate for different products. Sometimes different packaging for the same product works better in different geographic areas. There are many variables to consider. These same considerations apply to packaging yourself.

Like everybody else, I have strong personal preferences about clothing and fashion. I like certain things; I dislike other things. I'm sure you do, too. However, *the successful sales pro learns to set aside his or her preferences in favor of the most effective and appropriate personal packaging for a given situation.* You might think of this as image management. It is critically important.

A prime consideration when packaging yourself is the first impression you give others. Psychologists tell us that most people form impressions of others in the first four minutes of meeting them and that 80% of the impression is based on nonverbal input. What you say has very little to do with it. We also know that people are very reluctant to change their first impressions.

Another consideration is the overall, continuing impression you communicate. You need to always be thinking about what your appearance says about you.

Earlier I mentioned that The New Economy Customer is more discerning. That means he is, initially and continually, critically assessing and analyzing the salesperson or service provider or professional he's buying from or doing business with, alert for hints of what he can expect from the relationship going forward. What might have been overlooked, shrugged off, or assigned little importance during wildly free-spending times is now looked at and considered more seriously.

A Valuable Lesson from a Prejudiced Banker

Early in the operation of my first business—an ad agency—my Monday mail brought back a client's check for a sizable amount marked NSF. (That means "non-sufficient funds," although I'm told that in the South it means "not so fast!") This was not good news. So I jumped in my car and took my client's bad check to the bank, hoping there might be some money passing through that I could intercept. I sat down across the desk from the bank's vice president, passed him his customer's bad check, and told him my story.

The banker said, "As I'm sure you can appreciate, this is the type of matter we prefer to discuss only with the principals of the firms involved."

I handed him my business card and said, "I'm president of the agency. I'm the principal. Let's talk."

He said, in a sincerely surprised voice, "You *can't* be president; you're not wearing a tie."

Of course, I stomped and growled and slammed angrily out of the bank. But later, when I calmed down, I dealt with several interesting issues about success:

For Every One Person Who Says It, There Are Somewhere Between 10 and 10,000 Who Think It

All marketing research is based on that premise, and I believe it is sound. Most people are too intimidated or too lazy to express their opinions. Some are only subconsciously affected by something and couldn't enunciate their opinion even though their buying behavior is affected. Most companies count each customer complaint about a given product at 20 or 30 to 1, based on this premise. So the banker's notion about business leaders and neckties has much greater significance than just one solitary opinion from a banker with unfair preconceptions.

I do not like this fact, by the way. I wish image wasn't as important as it is. But fooling myself that way wouldn't be very smart. Comforting, but not smart. Comfortable, but not smart.

Of course, that incident occurred more than 30 years ago. We do live in more casual times. Maybe. Yet "image" seems more important than ever. And if I was going to bank or boardroom today to conduct important business, I would thoughtfully and meticulously choose personal packaging meant to make a particular statement. And it would include wearing of a tie.

In Selling, We Succeed Based on What Is, Not on What Ought to Be

I agree that books should not be judged by their covers. People should not be judged by the clothes they wear or the length of their hair. I argued that point vehemently when I was young and my hair was long. But I also know that the reality is that people do judge books and people by their covers.

I was at a social gathering this year and listened as the host's daughter, a recent high school graduate, complained bitterly to another guest, a doctor, about her experiences in the job market. She was dressed in a manner that can best be described as a cross between a rock musician and a homeless person. The doctor asked if she had gone out seeking employment dressed that way.

"Of course!" she replied. In fact, she had gone to apply for a job behind the counter at a yogurt shop—where she would be greeting customers and serving food to them—and been told that she could not work there looking like that. "How dare they try to tell me how I can dress?" she demanded, outraged at the injustice of the world.

Sadly, she is not alone in her stupidity.

Would You Rather Be Right or Rich?

I chose the latter, and I've learned to package myself as appropriately and effectively as possible for various situations—to fit the costume to the role. I assure you that it does make a difference.

In my speaking activities, I've experimented and satisfied myself that I sell my educational materials to a higher percentage of an audience when I'm wearing a suit than when I'm wearing a sports coat and slacks. Also, there are clothes I might wear in California that I will not wear in Massachusetts, for example. I've learned these things make a dollars-and-cents difference in my results.

There is no doubt in my mind that the clothes and accessories you wear, the briefcase you carry, the pen you write with, and the car you drive all combine to communicate a message to others that can help you or hurt you. To deny it, to resist it, or to ignore it is self-destructive.

Know this, too: people prefer dealing with successful people. I want my insurance agent, my real estate agent, my accountant,

> ## Dan Kennedy's #4 No B.S. Truth About Selling
>
> The logic is simple: if the packaging of products has an impact on how people regard those products, then the packaging of people must have an impact on how others regard those people.

my lawyer, my doctor, and my public relations consultant to be doing well. The fact that they appear to be doing well indicates that many others agree with my choice and my judgment.

I've also observed that I'm treated with greater courtesy and respect by merchants, store clerks, waiters and waitresses, bank tellers, airline employees, and hotel clerks when I'm dressed for business than when I'm in casual clothes.

To be absolutely honest, I no longer live this advice day-to-day, but then I no longer sell much; given that 90% of all my business is from continuing or repeat clientele, much of it done long-distance. I do dress casually when meeting with clients and running my coaching group meetings. I now live most of the time in a small town, and spend as much time as possible around the racetrack with my horses, so comfortable jeans and boots are the order of the day. But if I am speaking to a new audience, I break out the pin-striped suit, tie, and cuff links. On the now rare occasion when I travel to a new client's offices, on goes the tie, gray or tan slacks, blue blazer. I have a separate section in the closet for my "selling wardrobe."

Not long ago, I produced a television infomercial hosted by Robert Wagner. Younger people may only know him from the Austin Powers movies. You might also associate him with the popular *Hart to Hart* television series. Robert Wagner goes back to days of true Hollywood stars and classic leading men, like Cary Grant. He dresses this part. When we were discussing wardrobe, he said, "How 'bout if I wear my Basic TV Star Uniform?—Navy blue blazer, grey wool slacks, blue dress shirt, you pick the tie."

I believe in having the right uniform for the right role. When I go to sell, *I dress to sell.*

CHAPTER 6

STRATEGY 6
REMEMBERING WHY
YOU'RE THERE

This is an embarrassing confession:

One of the very first speaking engagements I ever had was for a client company at the opposite end of the country from my home. My compensation for speaking was to come solely from the sales of my books and audio learning programs to the audience; there was no fee being paid. Well, I went and spoke and I was a hit! The audience laughed uproariously, applauded enthusiastically, even gave me a standing ovation at the end. I was back on the plane, halfway home, having a celebratory drink when it dawned on me that I had completely forgotten about the products hidden under the podium. I had forgotten to give my commercial, forgotten to sell

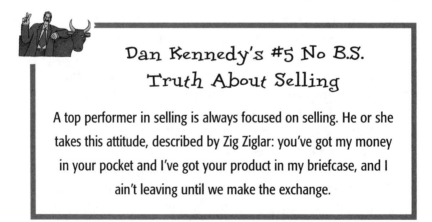

anything, even forgotten to bring the product back with me. *I had forgotten why I was there!*

I have been sharing this confession for years, and every time I tell it, it gets knowing reaction, rueful looks, nodding of heads. I've gotten letters specifically about it from readers of previous editions of this book. It seems everybody has caught themselves forgetting why they were there, at one time or another.

When the author of *Think and Grow Rich* Napoleon Hill wrote about **"definiteness of purpose,"** he was surely aiming his remarks at those of us involved in sales and marketing. *Clarity of purpose* is very valuable and very important in advertising, selling, negotiation, and communication. You need a clear, single objective.

Many professional salespeople resist this idea and, as a result, never rise above mediocre performance levels. They argue that they have to be concerned with creating and sustaining goodwill, building rapport, developing a friendly relationship, gathering information, and a myriad of other things in addition to selling. Unfortunately, they use these other things as excuses for nonperformance, as camouflage for a real problem—such as

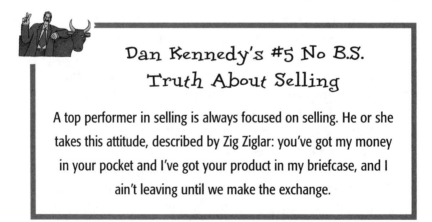

Dan Kennedy's #5 No B.S. Truth About Selling

A top performer in selling is always focused on selling. He or she takes this attitude, described by Zig Ziglar: you've got my money in your pocket and I've got your product in my briefcase, and I ain't leaving until we make the exchange.

the fear of asking for the order. Some salespeople muddle along as "professional visitors."

Of course, all those other things are important. Gathering information. Building rapport. But they should support selling, not distract from it or delay it. The New Economy demands efficiency and productivity, punishes waste. Ultimately, the sales professional must judge his effectiveness by whether or not he sells . . . at every opportunity.

One of the people I made a point of studying, to bolster my persuasive skills in general and my ability to sell to groups from the platform in specific, was Glenn W. Turner, the very controversial founder of Koscot, a cosmetics company, and Dare To Be Great, a self-improvement training company. The two companies together attracted an estimated 500,000 people in just three years to multi-level selling operations (after the fact ruled illegal pyramid selling operations)—largely through his remarkably powerful speeches. In his time, Glenn Turner was an international phenomenon, receiving immense media attention.

Glenn Turner, by the way, has a speech impediment. He was then and still is pretty difficult to listen to. In his early days in selling, he even had trouble getting hired for straight commission to sell sewing machines door-to-door. Certainly, nobody would pick him as one of the most persuasive public speakers and salespeople of all time.

But there's a film of an old speech by Turner called "Challenge to America," in which he is speaking to an audience of distributors and prospective distributors for one of his companies. He looks right at them and at the camera and says: "It's a good thing I don't have a hold of you cause I'd reach in and extract that check right out of your pocket."

I often think about that piece of film as I enter a "get the check" situation. Is that too tough for you? Is that high pressure? Only if it's felt as such. If it seems coarse by today's standards, that speaks more to your own uncertainty and timidity than to anything else. Most salespeople are far more sensitive than the sensibilities of the marketplace require.

If you worry too much about peripheral issues—such as being liked, loved, or even respected, or if you "buy into" the other person's problems too much, or if you are overly sensitive to the risk of being perceived as overbearing—you'll have a lot of "friends" but not much money.

That's why I think that you've got to take the trendy sales training programs infused with healthy doses of sensitivity training and pop-psych-babble with a big, fat grain of salt. There's non-manipulative selling, nonconfrontational selling, consultative selling, no-closing selling. Most of this seems to get translated to timidity in the field, and to quote Zig Ziglar again, "Timid salespeople have skinny kids."

Today, in teaching and in using Group Presentation Marketing, I often remind myself: "Remember why you're there." I don't care how much they laugh or applaud; whether or not I get a standing ovation is of minor importance. What counts is the number of people who buy and the amount they buy. These are the real statistics, the real measurements of success.

In fact, I'll tell you a "secret" about speaking that very few speakers like to admit: It's surprisingly easy to get an audience to laugh, to applaud, even to give a standing ovation. You can be a mediocre speaker and still engineer those results. So the speaker who takes great pride in "audience ratings" is either foolish or pretentious. In contrast, it's a lot harder to get 50%, 60%, 70%, 80%, even 90% of the people in an audience to reach into their pockets, pull out their hard-earned money, and spend it on your materials. To accomplish that, you have to deliver a greater quantity of better quality information with greater skill and charisma in order to get those results than you do just to get applause—*and* have a well structured sales presentation—*and* remember why you're there.

For 10 of the 30 years of my speaking career, I appeared on publicly promoted seminar programs with Zig Ziglar, and numerous celebrities in virtually every major U.S. and Canadian city, with several thousand people to as many as 35,000 in each audience. As the last speaker, I followed the last famous person, and usually had the 5:00 P.M. to 6:00 P.M. or 6:00 P.M. to 7:00 P.M. time slot. The audience had been there since 7:00 A.M. or 8:00 A.M., sitting on hard bleachers or stadium seats in arenas. As I walked on stage, they were poised to leave. Yet, even under these challenging circumstances, I routinely sold $50,000.00 to $75,000.00 worth of my books and audio learning programs each time and every time. How? Because I was totally focused on one objective and one objective only: making sales. Every word, every story in my presentation had been carefully chosen and assembled to make sales. The only measurement of my success I was interested in or paid any attention to was the number of sales.

The reason very few speakers ever become top performers in Group Presentation Marketing, why very few salespeople become high performers in their fields, is because they avoid putting themselves totally on the line for instant, measurable results. In the business of selling, the most significant sales are made after the seventh or eighth call-back to the customer or client. I say this has a lot more to do with the salesperson than with the customer. It is the salesperson's reluctance to push for definite results—and risk an early ending to the possibility of a sale—that causes this statistic.

Most salespeople like to make themselves feel good by having a lot of "almost persuaded" prospects they're working on and calling back on. But not me. I'd much rather have a "no" than a "maybe." I'd rather know where I stand as quickly as possible, so that I can move on to the next potentially productive use of my time. When somebody says to me, "Let me think about it," I say:

- Let's think about it together, out loud. After all, two heads are better than one.
- What, specifically, do you need time to think about?

- When someone has to think over a decision like this, it usually means he or she doesn't yet have enough information with which to make a decision. Let's review what we do know to see what may be missing.

I push to get on with it, right then.

When selling my own services as a speaker or as a consultant, as quickly as possible, as early in the conversation as possible, I talk about my schedule and say, "Let's see if I can even fit you in this month" or "Do you have a date in mind? Over half of mine for the rest of the year are already booked." I'm "closing" in this way from the very start. The last 20 of my 30 years have been about "one-call closes," on the phone, or at in-person meetings, of sales ranging from about $20,000.00 to $2-million. I really hate think-it-overs. And I do not accept the premise that they are necessary.

Those who insist on thinking things over present to you just one more challenge: to determine whether or not you know why you're there, and whether or not you're strong enough to get what you came for. If you are clear on your purpose—for calling someone, meeting with someone, making a presentation—you'll have a big competitive edge over most of the rest of the world.

CHAPTER 7

STRATEGY 7
DO EXPECTATIONS
GOVERN RESULTS?

I t was a big surprise to me when I first discovered that many people actually go into situations expecting to lose.

When my friend Brendan Suhr was an assistant head coach with Chuck Daly, when he and Daly coached the then dominant Detroit Pistons, he was asked what the big difference was between them and other NBA teams. Brendan said that, unlike other organizations he'd been with, everybody with the Pistons genuinely and whole-heartedly *expected* to win every game. I got a nearly identical answer from Jimmy Johnson about the dominating Dallas Cowboys team he built and coached. In neither case, incidentally, was this a statement of arrogance, swagger, or empty positive thinking; it was reflection of diligent preparation, organization, and skill. **If you don't honestly expect to win, you're probably entering a selling situation with a customer you should not be investing your time in, or a situation for which you are not properly and thoroughly prepared.**

In very recent years, one of my activities, in my role as chief strategic advisor to Glazer-Kennedy Insider's Circle™ has been working with Bill Glazer on planning, choreographing, and establishing sales expectations for our two major, internationally attended Member-conferences held during each year. These are complex events, with many general and break-out sessions; celebrity guest speakers like Gene Simmons from KISS or Ivanka Trump, celebrity CEO's like Terry Jones from Travelocity, Peter Shea from Entrepreneur Media (this book's publisher), or Jim McCann from 1-800-Flowers; 1,000 to 1,500 attendees, meal functions, exhibits, dozens of seminar presenters—and sales activity, requiring decisions about appropriate resources to be offered, prices, offers, speakers' presentations, merchandise in the on-premises store, and expectations for every speaker, every offer, total purchasing per attendee, revenues per hour, day, in entirety, and more. Make no mistake, we take our responsibilities to these events' attendees very, very seriously, and go to extreme lengths to deliver exceptional, practical value—evidenced by more than 70% of attendees returning year to year, and uninterrupted year-to-year growth even in recession. But also, to be candid, we take our task of creating the maximum possible income from these events just as seriously. *We determine in advance precisely what we are expecting in sales results before going in.* We do *not* "do our best and hope for the best." The process is much more scientific, deliberate, and painstaking than hope.

It so happens I know hundreds of other people in the business of putting on seminars and conferences, and have many as clients, and I can tell you that they all envy the Glazer-Kennedy results. If we compare math, they are stunned. But there are reasons. And a big one is our *intention*.

I don't think most salespeople expect to "get the check" every time out. They expect to be put off, expect stalls, expect multiple meetings and presentations to be necessary, generally expect NOT to get successful results—and more often than not, they get what they expect. Many salespeople even lower their own expectations in advance as a perverse means of feeling better about their results.

I have been in those selling situations myself and with others, observed them making excuses in advance for poor performance, and work very hard to stop myself from doing so. Even when going into "hostile territory" or difficult selling situations, I always figure out strategy I can have confidence in, and go in expecting to win and win big.

I prefer, and consistently stick to, working with entrepreneurial clients. But in this case that I will tell you about, I was referred to a Fortune 500 corporation, to discuss taking on a complex advertising project for them. I was told by the executive who brought me in that the CEO, his V.P. of Marketing, and his ad agency folk who would be there all thought my kind of direct-response marketing was voodoo. I was told the CEO would never agree to my standard compensation, which adds royalties tied to results on top of fees. Frankly, most of the time I'm aware of such an unfriendly, ill-prepared environment, I simply refuse to go; I fortunately no longer need to try and convert the ignorant. But in this case, for several compelling reasons, I went. I could have gone in accepting the executive's cautions and either compromised my presentation and compensation demands, or braced myself for failure. I did neither. I did my homework, researched the CEO's background, the company's situation, its competition, and went in with strategy and information I felt would be compelling. And I walked out with a $100,000.00 retainer. I *intended* nothing less.

Expectations and intentions can impact entire organizations' results too. I once consulted with an industrial company with a sales force accustomed to six-to-eight month sales cycles, multiple meetings before closing a sale, and dealing with decisions by committees. They refused to hear the message that their extended sales cycle was the result of their own expectations. About a year later I had the opportunity to consult with their chief competitor, a company half their size, experiencing the exact same frustrations, but blessed with a relatively open-minded president and sales team. We designed a radically different "top-down" marketing strategy targeting the CEOs of their prospect companies, intended to go from zero to a closed sale in a maximum of three meetings, over just three months. In just three years, this company surpassed its previously larger competitor in sales and size, averaging only 48 days from first contact to contract with new accounts.

My speaking colleague Mike Vance, a former close working associate of Walt Disney, tells of consulting with a company, asking the CEO to name his most vexing problem, getting the answer, then asking: "Who's working on solving it?"

"No one, " answered the CEO, "because it cannot be solved."

Unfortunately that doesn't just describe CEO behavior. It describes "stuck" sales managers and salespeople too.

Here's what I've come to devoutly believe: a marketing and selling system or process can be devised to achieve virtually any desired result or expectation. You start with the way you want

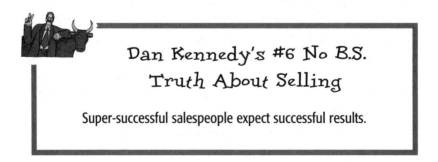

Dan Kennedy's #6 No B.S. Truth About Selling

Super-successful salespeople expect successful results.

things to occur, then work backward to put in place whatever is necessary to make it so.

Many people respond to an unsuccessful effort by saying, "I didn't expect that to happen anyway." I say, "Then why did you waste any effort on it? If you don't honestly expect success today, why not just roll over and go back to sleep?"

But let's be clear about this: I'm not talking about groundless, unreasonable expectations built out of "positive thinking" and nothing else. I'm talking about expecting success because you've created reasons to expect success.

Here's how I approach a selling or negotiating situation. First, I anticipate the worst—and carefully think through the ways that I may be able to counter or overcome the predictable, possible obstacles. Then, I expect the best. Often I visualize the entire process, rehearsing the entire dialogue in my head once, twice, even several times before actually proceeding with the meeting. I sell myself on the likelihood of getting what I want. And I believe this to be a vitally important sale to make. I've always done my best in selling, person to person or to groups, when I could make the actual selling experience déjà vu. By that I mean, it was con- structed in my mind and on paper in advance, with component parts from previous successful selling experiences; assembled into a complete mental movie; played over and over again until existing as clear expectation; then when actually experienced, it's déjà vu. These self-management techniques are from the afore- mentioned Dr. Maxwell Maltz' famous *Psycho-Cybernetics*.

In contrast, I find too many sales professionals just jumping into selling situations thoughtlessly, recklessly, ill-prepared, unrehearsed, with no right to reasonably expect great results. For example, I have clients who sell by tele-seminars who just show up to the call and "wing it." If I'm selling, I never do such an irre- sponsible thing. In fact, I write the entire teleseminar out on paper as a script. Edit it. Re-write it. Deliver it mentally before actually.

I have long used the same process for important selling situations. As example, when I set out to sell a division of one of my companies to a competitor, I used this process. I mention this example because it involved difficult obstacles and circumstances. The business I wanted to divest was troubled and that was no secret. There was the reasonable possibility the competitor could wait patiently and let us disappear from his landscape, without giving us a penny. Our technology was antiquated. And I had no significant flexibility in price or terms; there was a number I had to have, and I had to be paid immediately.

I thought through all the reasons it made good sense for them to accept the proposition—from their point of view. I thought through the possible reasons not to do the deal, and developed answers to them. I played out the entire meeting in my imagination, what Dr. Maltz terms the "Theater of Your Mind." By the time I sat down with them in the first meeting I had every expectation of successfully consummating the deal. In fact, I was a little surprised when I walked out without a definite yes and had to wait a couple of weeks to complete the transaction. However, in the selling of companies, two weeks from zero to finish line is breakneck speed.

Expectation is a powerful force. This concept is described by Napoleon Hill in his book *Think and Grow Rich*: "Whatever the mind of man can conceive and **believe**, it can achieve." (Emphasis is mine.) "Believe" is the key word in this equation. You have to believe your proposition before anyone else will. You have to believe, with reason, that you will secure acceptance now, not later. And I am convinced that when your belief reaches 100%, you are guaranteed acceptance by the other person—the customer, client, whomever.

Persuasion involves transferring your feelings onto the other person. If you "secretly" feel—

- I'm not very good at persuading others
- He's too smart to fall for this . . . he'll never go for this

- He's a much better, much more experienced negotiator
- I wish this problem didn't exist with this deal
- I hope he hasn't gotten a quote from XYZ, too; I can't beat their prices

then you'll "transmit" those feelings to the other person, and it could affect the response. He may become uncomfortable, hesitant, insecure, and reluctant to proceed. And he may not consciously know why either, saying, "It's just a feeling" or offering a vague justification for delay.

On the other hand, when you do feel that the proposition is at least as good for the other party as it is for you, when you feel that the other person would be smart to say yes and stupid to say no, when you feel that you have something to offer that is better than anything available from any other source, and when you feel that you are as good at communicating all of that as anyone could possibly be—you transfer those feelings, too. When you genuinely expect favorable and immediate response, you communicate that expectation.

There are many professional salespeople with tremendous ability, extensive knowledge of their products, good selling skills, comprehensive training and education, and excellent opportunities who fail miserably, repetitively. Why? There is just one ingredient missing in their situation: conviction—the belief in themselves and their proposition, the expectation of successful outcome.

Unfortunately, the experience of recession—worsened by media hype and political posturing and misery-loves-company conversation—convinced a great many business owners and sales professionals to lower and shrink their expectations about what they could sell at what prices, to whom, how quickly. They carry those pre-set expectations with them into every selling situation, regardless of the individual prospect's situation or the changes in the economy. At the time you read this book, the expectations of price resistance and buying resistance from all customers may very well be greater and more controlling in most salespeople's minds than at any time since the Depression of the 1930s.

Even at the deepest point of this current or most recent recession, such expectations were not warranted by facts, especially if the salesperson practiced sound strategies for choosing good prospects (discussed later in this book). People bought and made immediate buying decisions—even at premium prices—*every single day*. In fact, the very day the stock market crashed below 8,000 the first time in this recession, a friend of mine and I dined at Ill Molino, a breathtakingly expensive restaurant. Every table was full. Our waiter showed no hesitation whatsoever in offering us pricey, extra appetizers, exotic cheeses, top-priced liquor. No one there decided there was no point in opening that night or no point in even trying to sell the most extravagant extras, and there was clear expectation of acceptance—they brought the goodies to the table and asked for the sale simultaneously. I was impressed by what I saw them doing, and at how successful they were at transforming the attitude of those entering, from shell-shocked, anxious, beaten (and no doubt resistant to spending) to upbeat, energized, involved, and happy to spend.

In The New Economy, my expectation is for the expectations of those selling goods, services, and, preferably, experiences to matter more than ever before. New Economy Customers will have come through a series of experiences and a period of time that has damaged their willingness to trust anyone or anything, dampened their optimism, and made them more circumspect. Early in 2009, ten years of accumulated stock market gains were wiped out in fewer than 30 days. The national debt was either doubled or tripled, depending on what you want to include or leave off-books, virtually overnight. Institutions viewed as rock-sold, like America's biggest banks, its auto-makers, blue chip corporations, were revealed as weak, vulnerable, and deceptive phantoms. Consumers and business owners alike have been shaken to their core. Even as a strong, albeit strong in different ways, New Economy replaces the old, the emotional and psychological scars will not easily or quickly heal and disappear. The New Economy Customer will need to borrow strength, confidence, and certainty via transference of feeling from those who sell to him, those he chooses to buy from.

CHAPTER 8

STRATEGY 8
PROOF: THE MOST IMPORTANT TOOL FOR EXCEPTIONAL SUCCESS IN SELLING

I am about to reveal to you—and attempt to sell you on—the single most important, most powerful selling tool that exists. That's a big claim. I know that. Yet I have personally seen this single tool transform losing businesses into huge successes, and mediocre salespeople into superstars. I have used it myself many different times, many different ways, for great profit.

First, a story:

One afternoon I was visiting the offices of a famous, very successful criminal attorney. By that, I do not mean he was a criminal. He represents people alleged to be criminals. Admittedly, a thin line. Anyway, he and several of his associates were gathered in the firm's conference room discussing a trial that was to begin the following day. He was asking his associates for their comments about their ability to win their client's acquittal.

The client had the risk of serving at least 20 years, possibly longer, in a federal prison should these lawyers fail. In the client's favor was the fact that this particular lawyer very rarely lost a case.

The attorney asked his associates for their comments, and a young lawyer spoke up: "I'm confident that we have gathered enough proof for you to prove his innocence if necessary."

The attorney came up out of his chair, lunged across the conference table, grabbed his young associate by the neck, and pulled him out of his chair, so that they were almost nose-to-nose. He then said, in a deadly voice: "Don't ever send me into a courtroom with 'enough' proof. I want a preponderance of proof."

I have never forgotten the importance of that lesson. Having a preponderance of proof makes it possible to sell with 100% effectiveness, 100% of the time. If you want to win with every presentation of every proposition, make sure you have an overwhelming amount of proof that what you are selling is a great

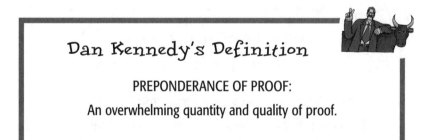

Dan Kennedy's Definition

PREPONDERANCE OF PROOF:
An overwhelming quantity and quality of proof.

deal, have an overwhelming quality of proof, and have proof that is influential. Influential proof directly addresses the anxieties, doubts, concerns, skepticisms, interests, hopes, and desires of the individual prospect.

Proof Through Testimonials

I have now done work with clients in over 250 different product and service categories, from weight loss and cosmetic dentistry to investments to funeral homes to custom-fabricated parts for nuclear power plants. And I have yet to find one business—not one—where using testimonials as proof hasn't substantially improved sales. Yet 90% of all the sales professionals I encounter—those who try selling to me, those I am hired to observe and train, those who seek me out for assistance—either completely fail to use testimonials or use them sparingly and poorly.

If you did nothing else as a result of this book but ten times your use of testimonials in "proving your case" to your prospects, your reading time will produce a huge return on investment.

Testimonial letters and comments can be used in sales and marketing in many different ways. They can be used in advertising,

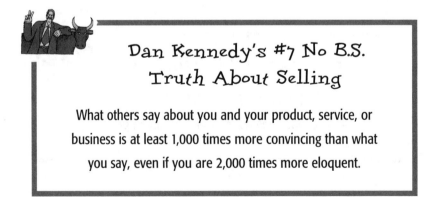

Dan Kennedy's #7 No B.S. Truth About Selling

What others say about you and your product, service, or business is at least 1,000 times more convincing than what you say, even if you are 2,000 times more eloquent.

direct mail, and promotional literature. They can be used as part of a one-on-one or group sales presentation. They can be given to the client to read. They can be put in a big notebook and kept in the waiting room or reception area for people to browse through. They can be videotaped and put up on a website, played on a laptop in a one-on-one setting.

In my experience, there is nothing more valuable than a great testimonial letter—other than two great testimonial letters!

In The New Economy, proof-by-customers' testimonies rises to a whole new level of importance for reasons I just enumerated at the end of the previous chapter and elsewhere in this book.

At the end of this chapter, I've included one of the best demonstrations of truly powerful testimonials I've ever had one of my clients create. His name is Paul Johnston, and he owns Shed Shop Inc., a company that sells backyard sheds. This is a rather ordinary product made extraordinary through the emotion-laded, human interest stories collected from satisfied customers and published in a booklet, titled "83 Practical Uses for a Shed Shop Shed." I originally suggested this to Paul as a "Chicken Soup for the Shed Shop Owner's Soul" type of story book, mimicking the hugely successful approach taken by my friend Mark Victor Hansen, co-creator of the multimillion best-selling phenomenon, the actual *Chicken Soup for the Soul* book series. Paul executed the idea brilliantly. I'll let him tell you of the results in his own words:

> "At a marketing conference for his Members in 1999, Dan was drilling into us the importance of using testimonials. I mentioned that our customers were always telling us interesting, unusual, even heart-warming stories about how they used our sheds, and Dan said I could do a book of them. And I did.
>
> To get the stories, we held a contest for the most creative or unusual use for a Shed Shop shed, invited our customers to submit stories and photos, and awarded prizes. We

wound up with a booklet titled "83 Practical Uses for a Shed Shop Shed," containing the 83 best stories.

We send this booklet to every prospect. The impact was immediate and dramatic. Selling became much easier, as the customers were pre-sold on doing business with us, and more eager to talk with us about why they wanted a backyard shed. This supported an increase in our prices, it sets us apart from competitors, it helps sell add-on options. I now think of it as my million dollar story-book!"

That was in 1999. Since then, the "emotional testimonial storybook"—and extensions of it into various media—has become a staple of selling. I've taught it to and had it used by thousands in every imaginable field, from operators of pizza shops to marketers of sophisticated software systems enabling mid-sized companies. In the latter case, it's not testimony about what the software does that makes the story; it's what the mid-sized company's owners feel when they make the *Inc.* 500 List of fastest growth companies for the first time thanks to use of the software. In the case of the pizza shop, it's not a customer talking about the pizza; it's the customer talking about getting the entire family together once a month for pizza night, and what that means to her.

The New Economy is all about personal, emotional connection, so this can only matter more and more.

How Dumb Salespeople Work Ten Times Harder Than They Need To and Get One-Tenth the Results They Could Get

If you under-utilize testimonials, there you are, huffing, puffing, straining, and struggling to convey your marketing message and convince of your virtues, while you keep an entire army of more persuasive, more instantly believable salespeople eager to do the heavy lifting for you for free, bound and gagged, locked in the closet, out of sight.

How dumb is that?

If you fail to utilize emotional connection story testimonials, you're taxed with the entire task of trying to link your company, product, service, and deliverables to customers' feelings, while sitting on the sidelines, silent, are people able to tell the prospect exactly how they feel thanks to using your product.

Aren't their stories certain to connect better than your promises?

On the next page of this chapter, you will find a sign I gave to all my Members back in 2002. It is copyrighted, but you have my permission to photocopy the page as much as you like for your own use or for others in your sales organization. Stick it up places you'll see it often to nag you as I would in person if I could.

A Picture Is Worth a Thousand Words

Another incredibly powerful type of proof is pictorial. The cliché is true: a picture is worth a thousand words. Pictorial proof is interesting and novel, it communicates at a glance, and it has lasting impact. Your camera could be your best friend in sales! Now, of course, it's ridiculously easy to take photos or get guerilla videos of your customers in their habitats using your products—the phone you carry probably shoots both. And you can upload it all to your website. And so on. You have all this nifty technology at your disposal, how about using it for something other than taking pictures of the squirrels drinking out of your hot tub for You-Tube?

Let's go way back in time. The late Ira Hayes, a former top National Cash Register (NCR) salesman, used this technique when he started selling cash registers to small shop owners, when the cash register was a new "technology," replacing the

"Let THEM
Say It For You."

© 2002/D.S. Kennedy. www.dankennedy.com

"Let THEM
Say It For You."

© 2002/D.S. Kennedy. www.dankennedy.com

"Let THEM
Say It For You."

© 2002/D.S. Kennedy. www.dankennedy.com

cigar box under the counter. Yes, imagine that—there was a time when the cash register was a revolutionary piece of equipment looked upon with suspicion, and that time was within my lifetime. He had a 20 to 30 foot black fabric panel that he carried with him. On that panel were thousands of snapshots of happy, satisfied customers standing next to their shiny new cash register. Hayes would take this giant "wall" of snapshots into a prospect's office and unfurl it impressively. The sale was made before the selling even started—because the proof was overwhelming.

Ira was once asked, when he was traveling and speaking to general business audiences such as Chamber of Commerce groups, sponsored by NCR, why NCR and he were so willing to reveal his selling secret. Ira answered: "We're not worried about our competitors' salespeople stealing this idea. We can't even get our own people to use it."

Another salesperson I've seen use it to a similar extent is a top Ford salesman in Phoenix. In his cubicle, the walls are covered with photographs, each showing a customer or a customer-family, smiling, standing next to their new Ford. Each photo is dated and has the customer's name on it. When I lived in Phoenix for about ten years, he was my car salesman and, through referrals, my family's and friends' car salesman. My photo was there, with my Lincoln. My brother's photo was there with his pickup truck. My father's photo was there, with his Mercury Marquis. And so on. Some families have many more photos there, from a series of vehicles they purchased over the years. It doesn't take too long to accept the pictures as proof that this guy treats his customers right—otherwise, how could he have so many of them?

Incidentally, I recently had reason to buy a Ford from another dealership in another state. I walked in and paid cash for a $35,000.00 SUV. I was never shown any testimonials, never asked for one, never asked for a referral either. Nor has there been one ounce of follow-up from that sales rep. The next year, in that state, I bought two cars—neither one from him.

Anyway, you can use "photo proof" in any type of business. A retail store might take pictures of happy customers with their newly purchased merchandise. A lawn service company might photograph the customers' yards and gardens. A florist might photograph the happy, surprised recipients of delivered flowers. In my literature, I often use the photos taken of me with famous people: actors and actresses I've worked with in infomercials, athletes, coaches, even former U.S. Presidents I've appeared on seminar programs with. Give some thought to how you can apply this principle to your business.

Statistical Proof

Statistics provide a third impressive form of proof. For example, I surveyed a group of entrepreneurs who were using my audio learning programs one year, and I've since shown the survey results to hundreds and hundreds of audiences. The results conclude that:

- 98% reported satisfaction
- 83% reported improved sales
- 87% made additional purchases

At my suggestion, many of my clients who put on annual seminars and conferences survey the attendees months afterward, and document the average income increase achieved— often from $40,000.00 to $100,000.00, and then use that fact as a powerful sales tool for subsequent seminars—*proving* that it's not costing you $3,000.00 to come, it's costing you $40,000.00 to stay home. This supports a particular type of direct-mail piece I like these clients to use, with a very realistic looking and feeling faux check, made out to each prospect by name, for $40,000.00 enclosed, along with a form designed for the business owner and

Other Proof

Consider these ideas for evidence you might use:

Traditional

- Customer or client lists
- Length of time in business
- Past credentials, qualifications, experience
- Financial references
- Number of cities/countries serviced
- Number of customers served
- Physical demonstrations, "live" or on video
- "Flip Books," Binders, or Power Points presentations of testimonials used in face-to-face selling

Untraditional

- "Story books"
- Infomercial-style testimonial videos
- Audio CD's with interviews with testimonials
- Toll-free 800-number "eavesdrop lines" to hear what clients or customers have called in and recorded about your product or service
- Testimonial letters, photos, etc. presented in a website

spouse to plan what they'll buy or do with the extra $40,000.00. This is a creative way to present statistical proof, and to get the prospect involved with it.

How Much Proof Is Enough?
How Much Proof Is Too Much?

There is no such thing as enough; no such thing as too much. It is better to have more than you need rather than less.

I can't tell you how many salespeople and businesspeople I have taught this to, yet it is still a well-kept secret. No one else at the car dealership where the car salesman I described works will use the ideas, even though he has been a star, award-winning, high-income performer. Even though I've taught the same photo and photo + testimonial display technique to at least 10,000 chiropractors, dentists, and cosmetic surgeons, 9,900 won't do it.

It's not your job, though, to worry about why others won't use these techniques. Their resistance is your opportunity! Successful people do the things that unsuccessful people are unwilling to do. If you choose to join the successful minority, you'll discover that most of the things you do to get results— even if openly shared with others—will rarely be copied and used by others. For that reason, the use of *preponderance of proof* as the core of selling or advertising or marketing remains a best-kept, immensely valuable secret.

FIGURE 8.1: The Shed Stories

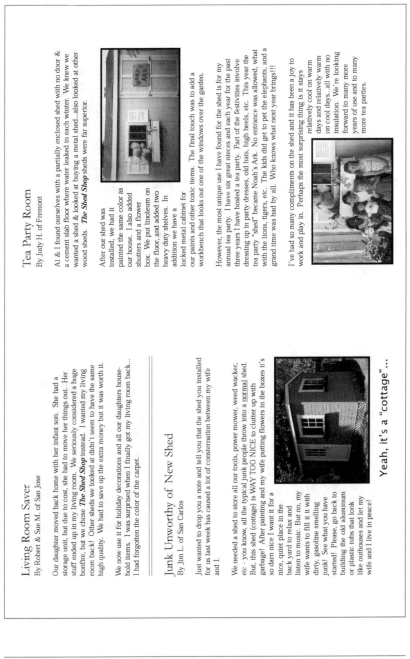

Living Room Saver
By Robert & Sue M. of San Jose

Our daughter moved back home with her infant son. She had a storage unit, but due to cost, she had to move her things out. Her stuff ended up in my living room. We seriously considered a huge bonfire, but we chose *The Shed Shop* instead. I wanted my living room back! Other sheds we looked at didn't seem to have the same high quality. We had to save up the extra money but it was worth it.

We now use it for holiday decorations and all our daughters household items. I was surprised when I finally got my living room back... I had forgotten the color of the carpet.

Junk Unworthy of New Shed
By Jim L. of San Carlos

Just wanted to drop you a note and tell you that the shed you installed for us last week has caused a lot of consternation between my wife and I.

We needed a shed to store all our tools, power mower, weed wacker, etc - you know, all the typical junk people throw into a normal shed. But, this shed (cottage) is WAY TOO NICE to clutter up with garbage! After painting and my wife putting flowers in the boxes it's so darn nice I want it for a nice, quiet place in the back yard to relax and listen to music. But no, my wife wants to fill it with junk! See what you have started! Please, go back to building the old aluminum or plastic tubs that look like outhouses and let my wife and I live in peace!

Yeah, it's a "cottage"...

Tea Party Room
By Judy H. of Fremont

Al & I found ourselves with a partially enclosed shed with no door & a cement slab floor where water leaked in each winter. We knew we wanted a shed & looked at buying a metal shed...also looked at other wood sheds. *The Shed Shop* sheds were far superior.

After our shed was installed, we had it painted the same color as our house. I also added shutters and a flower box. We put linoleum on the floor, and added two heavy duty shelves. In addition we have a locked metal cabinet for our paints and other toxic items. The final touch was to add a workbench that looks out one of the windows over the garden.

However, the most unique use I have found for the shed is for my annual tea party. I have six great nieces and each year for the past three years I have hosted a tea party. Part of the festivities involve dressing up in party dresses, old hats, high heels, etc. This year the tea party "shed" became Noah's Ark. No entrance was allowed, what with the lions, tigers, etc. The kids did get to pet the elephants, and a grand time was had by all. Who knows what next year brings!!!

I've had so many compliments on the shed and it has been a joy to work and play in. Perhaps the most surprising thing is it stays relatively cool on warm days and relatively warm on cool days...all with no insulation. We're looking forward to many more years of use and to many more tea parties.

FIGURE 8.1: The Shed Stories, continued

Singer's Studio
By Gary M. of Grizzly Flats

My wife, Jackie and I are both singers (we met as members of the Northern CA Vocal Artists Association). Our karaoke equipment, including hundreds of background tapes, had not had a separate room since we moved to Grizzly Flats in September 1996. The equipment was in our bedroom. Our guest room and our office were too small and adding another room onto the house would have been far too costly.

A separate shed was the ideal solution as it provides for a designated room and we don't bother our 8-year-old daughter Tabby. In comparing *The Shed Shop* with other companies it was clear *The Shed Shop* was the best. Even though it was the most expensive, the quality of your shed more than made up for this "negative."

We had a contractor put in electricity, insulation, and walls. We have all of our equipment, tapes, and CD's in the shed in addition to music-related pictures on the walls.

I'm singing my 50's-60's rock-n-roll and Jackie her show and other songs. It's great! Should we get more than one room full of company, the futon in the shed will sleep 2 adults or 3-4 children. I can also see patients there if anyone wants to come to Grizzly Flats (I'm a psychotherapist). My satisfaction has been complete thus far.

Singin' in the trees...

Parental Storage
By Julie N. of Alamo

A move from Idaho resulted in a smaller house & garage but a bigger fixer-upper yard. Storage was very tight. An old shed served only to house black widows & stray rain drops. Anything in the old shed turned green and mushy.

Other alternatives included an expansion of the garage... impractical & expensive. *Shed Shop* sheds were charming and priced right. Customer service was great... knowledgeable, quick & efficient. I wish all California builders were this good! Do you do houses??

Our new shed houses garden equipment; saddles I will never part with...despite what my husband says; dog houses that the new dog will not enter. I even kidded with my parents I would store them in there when they "retired." They were OK with that because it is so cute.

It has become "yard art!!" We jazzed it up with antique accents. It adds charm to our views. We even planted our shed its own cute little garden.

Mom & dad's retirement home?

FIGURE 8.1: The Shed Stories, continued

Computer Room
By Lisa D. and family of Livermore

Just wanted you to see another variation on your wonderful sheds. My family and I have converted it into a computer room to free up a bedroom for our new baby boy.

We all spend most evenings in here and are surprised at how roomy and comfortable it is. We currently house 3 computers (9 hard drives total), a TV, 3 VCR's, a scanner, 2 printers, a fax machine and MORE. And it all fits so nicely in 120 square feet.

All of our friends think it's great! And we saved about $50,000 dollars when compared to a room/house addition! We have had no problems with our shed. Thanks again for a wonderful product!

Peanut Shack
By Don S. of San Jose

Our shed is a multipurpose building that houses old paint, sprayers, teak furniture, and peanuts for visiting squirrels. It definitely holds more peanuts for my squirrels than I realized! We are 100% satisfied with *The Shed Shop.*

For visiting squirrels...

Recreational Equipment Filled My Garage
By Dave C. of Palo Alto

Our garage was crowded with all your typical outdoor stuff...bikes, skateboards, roller blades, & other recreational equipment. Not enough room left for the cars!!

We tried garage organizers, shelving, storage hooks, etc. But it was still crowded and difficult to access both the equipment and cars.

I chose *The Shed Shop* over others due to: 1) quality design/materials/construction; 2) friendly staff; 3) ability to have shed built-to-order; 4) ability to drive & see samples on their lot. It now houses all our outdoor stuff.

While your prices weren't the lowest, this was the best value: quality, attractive, great team. I've recommended you to several friends & neighbors!!

Cars In, Filing Cabinets Out!
By Terri C. of San Ramon

My home business requires that I keep client files from prior years in my garage in 4 filing cabinets. When we bought a new car, we needed to now park our 3 cars in the garage...the filing cabinets needed to go!

To solve the problem, we chose a shed from *The Shed Shop* for their great looks and sturdy construction. The shed is easily seen by our neighbor so we didn't want to create an eyesore for them. The filing cabinets are now in the shed as are our earthquake supplies & water.

As a joke to one neighbor (who has no shed), another neighbor (who also has a shed) and I hung Christmas lights on our sheds in July. Our "in-between" neighbor really enjoyed the festive look of the shed & we all had a good laugh.

FIGURE 8.1: The Shed Stories, continued

Family Heirloom
By Dale, Nancy, & Kelsey S. of Fremont

Last spring we visited some model homes in Sacramento and in one of the backyards there was a little playhouse set up. Our daughter Kelsey fell in love with it and all she could do was talk about how "cool" it was. We had previously thought about getting her a play-house, but decided we didn't want to spend that much money for something she would outgrow in a few years.

Then we heard about *The Shed Shop*. Here was a product that looked cute enough for a playhouse, yet could be used as a storage shed when Kelsey outgrew it. When we stopped in, a very nice woman explained everything about the sheds and what options were available. We decided on an extra window, dutch door, and flower box.

We wrapped up a **Shed Shop** brochure in half birthday and half Christmas paper and gave it to Kelsey at dinner. The look on her face was priceless. While waiting for the delivery date she talked non stop about all she would doing in it. She picked out paint colors (yellow, purple, and green), curtains, house numbers, mailbox, park bench, bookshelf, welcome mat, and carpet.

Kelsey has spent many hours in the playhouse using her imagination and having fun. We're sure as she grows the playhouse will be changed from a home for her dolls into a teenage refuge full of beanbag chairs and boomboxes. We hope this playhouse will be part of our family forever. We imagine our grandchildren coming to visit someday and telling them about the fun we had with their mom putting the playhouse together...and then watching them play in it too.

Workshop and Storage
By Yolanda P. of San Lorenzo

We had an old metal shed in the back yard that was too small and was falling apart, it was rusting away. For two years things were piling up in the garage and patio area. There was no other alternative to getting a new shed. We just had to decide what size, when to purchase, and who to buy it from. Once we visited *The Shed Shop* and saw some of the displays, we were totally convinced that this was the way to go.

Our new shed is being used as a work shop and storage area. A work bench has been built and shelf installed in the shed. Some of the stored items include fishing rods, camping equipment, and mountain bikes. With the new shed our garage and patio area is neater and cleaner looking. Your people did a great job from start to finish, keep up the good work.

Great use of wall space!

Santa's Workshop
By Karen W. of Redwood City

Our garage had been turned into our family room years ago and storage space has always been a huge problem. I liked the looks of a wooden structure in the yard since it is readily seen from the house.

I plan to decorate the shed at Christmas as Santa's Workshop. My husband does look like Santa, too! We're using it for storage of all kinds of supplies, extra Costco purchases, Christmas tree and other holiday decorations. I didn't expect it to be such an addition to the looks of the yard - see picture.

CHAPTER 9

STRATEGY 9
FRED HERMAN'S
K.I.S.S. PRINCIPLE

E arl Nightingale once called the late Fred Herman "America's greatest sales trainer." It's a title I think he deserved. To my knowledge, Fred is the only salesman ever to appear as a guest on *The Tonight Show* with Johnny Carson. (Carson said, "OK, since you're the greatest salesman, sell me this ashtray." Fred picked it up, examined it, and asked, "If you were going to buy this ashtray, what would you expect to pay for it?" Carson named a price. Fred said, "Sold!")

I discovered Fred Herman's work after I already had years of experience in selling; I wish I had found it when I started. Fred is probably most famous for coining the KISS Principle for Selling: **KEEP IT SIMPLE, SALESMAN!** This is an immensely valuable lesson that I learned the hard way.

In my first sales position, with the publishing company I described earlier in this book, one of the things I was most effective at was opening new accounts where we could place the entire six-foot-tall spinner rack. The standard procedure prescribed by the company was to review the catalog of books with the buyer, choosing the titles to be displayed in the rack. As the rack only held about one-third of all the available titles, this selection process was a time-consuming chore. The customer and I had to discuss just about every title. Inevitably, he or she wanted more variety than the rack could accommodate. I found it took almost two hours, on average, to place a new rack.

Then I realized that almost 90% of the racks I placed carried the same titles on them. So I reasoned that I knew better than the customer which titles would do best, and I was wasting his or her time and mine discussing products that would not be on the rack. From this realization, I created a "standard rack assortment" which I copied and used every time I sold a new customer a rack. All the customer had to do was initial the precompleted form and I was on my way. Average time savings: 90 minutes per new rack placement!

How come nobody else in the company had thought of this?

People have an incredible tendency to complicate their lives. I'm not sure why that happens, but I know that it happens. I even have a name for it: complexity creep. Complexity just creeps up on you when you're not looking. And, unnecessary complexity creates a whole host of problems. It wastes time, it drains your energy and enthusiasm, it often confuses the customer—and confused customers do not buy!

The New Economy's Chaos of Choices and New Economy Customers' Desire for the Easy Button

There's an excellent book by Barry Schwartz, *The Paradox of Choice*, that explains the ever-growing unhappiness of most consumers as their choices in every category of product and service expand exponentially. You might think more choices would make people happier, but that's not the case. Having 10 brands of designer shoes to choose from instead of 3 does; having 200 does not. I happen to like soup, and I find myself confused by the dizzying and ever-growing choices just within the Campbell's brand. This past year they premiered V-8 soups by Campbell's, and for the life of me, I don't know why the V-8/Campbells vegetable soup is different or superior or inferior to the regular Campbell's vegetable or their premium vegetable or their Select Harvest vegetable, and to be honest I find all that more thinking than I care to do, just to buy some soup. So I haven't bought any in months. If only there was a really good soup salesman to guide me to precisely the perfect soup for me—given that I am diabetic, I am in my 50s, I need a lot of energy for my work, I'm usually in a hurry so complex preparations are out, and price is no object.

In the emerging New Economy, one way companies are competing for business is to divide and conquer; even to compete with themselves; and keep bringing more and more and more choices of a product or service to market. This, however, is contrary to the New Economy Customer's time pressures from an always-connected, always-multitasking, always-on-the-run existence. One of the reasons the office products store chain's "Easy Button" ad campaign resonated with so many people and lasted as long as it did is this wish for simplicity.

There's never been a better time to do what I started doing 30+ years ago: simplifying the buyer's deciding for him.

If you can secure the trust of a customer, then he will welcome you *deciding for him.* This is why a sales strategy like the bundling together of multiple goods and services into one, two, or (no more than) three "packages" to choose from almost always out-perform cafeteria or a la carte offers, in terms of closing percentages and average transaction size.

You Can Get Rich
Making the Complicated Simple

I recently saw an interesting advertisement placed by a copy-writer looking for work. He billed himself as a "professional explainer" who specialized in "making complicated things simple and easy to understand." That's exactly what you need to do in your efforts to persuade others. (Too bad there's nobody who'll do that for me, for assembly directions for things I buy or for my damned computer.)

Not long ago, I was wrestling with a direct-mail project involving the sale of a rather complicated financial product to unsophisticated investors. Two consecutive test mailings failed miserably. I thought they were well-written, clear, and exciting. I thought they offered a great deal to the customer. I thought everything was right. Just one small problem: they didn't work. I read through them a hundred times and still found no clue to the problem. One evening, I got the idea to add a little diagram at the end of the literature that showed—in cartoon form—the gist of the product. The addition of this little drawing, which showed visually what was said in the copy, made the piece a huge success. The mailing with the drawing got phenomenally good results. That one little drawing made the complicated simple and understandable.

P.T. Barnum once said that, "No man ever went broke over-estimating the ignorance of the American public." Maybe that judgment of the American consumer is a little harsh, but it does introduce a major mistake made by the majority of sales and marketing people over and over again: overestimating the sophistication of their customers. New Economy Customers may have been conditioned by recession to try and be more circum-spect, but that does not mean they miraculously got smarter.

It's natural for you to insist that the people you deal with are smarter than everybody else's customers. That reflects well on you, doesn't it? It's good for your ego to think that you're dealing with a "better class" of people. It may be good for the ego, but it's bad for the bank account! Here is the best way to succeed in advertising, selling, marketing, or persuading others (regardless of who they are or how smart and sophisticated you believe they are): present *everything* in the simplest possible language and in the simplest possible form.

Close the Doors on the Sales *Prevention* Department

A lot of companies have a more active Sales Prevention Department than they do a sales operation—overrun with sales-killing policies, rules, laws, forms. Often this happens if the lawyers and bean-counters gain excess power back at the home office. I do not envy those of you working for the worst of these. My first and only sales job mentioned earlier in this chapter was with a company who had such a department, but even more so, had management focused on everything but the ease and simplicity with which an account could be opened, a new customer brought into the fold. I was able to circumvent the home office and invent my own streamlined, simplified sales process. Maybe you can too. But if you must try dragging the powers-that-be above you out of the sales prevention mode, here's a story that may help you sell your ideas. Feel free to use it as your own.

There's a little neighborhood, mom-n-pop coffee shop near my home, where I sometimes eat breakfast. On the counter, next to the cash register, there are three different receptacles for coins, for charitable donations—one for Kiwanis, one for something for the blind, one for disabled veterans. One morning, as I dropped my change into one of them, it registered with me that I *always* plunked my change into the same one. Why? I stood there for a few minutes, pondering my own behavior.

Then it hit me. The reason I *always* put my change into the disabled veterans jar was . . .

NOT because I had any preference for that charity over the others. NOT because of any reasoned decision to support it instead of the others.

NOT because of the graphic design or appearance of the different containers. NOT because of any sales copy on the containers. NOT because of their arrangement on the counter.

NOT for any thoughtful or logical or admirable reason. BUT definitely for a reason.

The reason, and the only reason, I put all my change into only one of these charity jars, each and every time, is . . .

the hole in the top of the jar I put all my coins into is bigger than the holes in the lids on the other two jars.

CHAPTER 10

STRATEGY 10
SELL MONEY AT
A DISCOUNT

This selling strategy is vital in The New Economy. A new sense of "responsible consumerism" has spread—or, if you take a very long view of history, returned—and people now need more sensible, defensible justifications for buying what they want to buy, and what you want to sell to them. The good news is that almost anything can be sold to anybody at any time, if there is desire for it on their part, and if you have a sufficiently compelling money-at-a-discount story to tell. It is *imperative* that you develop ways to make yours a money-at-discount proposition.

I was once retained as a consultant to an individual who lectured on methods of preventing theft from employees and vendors' delivery staff. This individual was a reformed thief who knew how it was done from having done it. (This kind of theft is a little-known problem of huge magnitude. In the typical convenience store, for example, the theft equals or even exceeds the owner's profit.)

This expert ex-thief was teaching business owners how to prevent this sort of loss—and they were thrilled. In fact, he had boxes full of testimonial letters from store owners and executives citing specific amounts of money saved in the weeks or months following his seminar. These letters documented the saving of thousands of dollars per store. Some big companies reported savings of as much as $100,000.00 in just a couple of months by applying what they learned.

He had no idea what he was worth. He was charging only $500.00 to conduct his all-day seminar, and he had one little reference notebook with six audio recordings that recapped the seminar, simply packaged in a bag, that he was selling for about $30.00.

Let me confess: this was the easiest marketing task I ever had. The first thing I suggested was that he raise his fees. In fact, I convinced him to triple his fee from $500.00 to $1,500.00 immediately. To his shock (but not mine) there was very little protest and no loss of clients. Shortly after that, the fee was raised again to $2,500.00 with just a little client grumbling. Even at $2,500.00 a day, he was such a bargain that no one could afford to grumble too much. In essence, we were now selling up to $100,000.00 for $2,500.00. Who wouldn't buy that? And we had the proof to demonstrate it. Within a year, his fee was $7,500.00, and then doubled to $15,000.00, and he was still attracting more business than he could handle.

I based his entire marketing program on *proving that he was offering money at a discount.* In other words, we showed the prospect such a large, compelling return on investment that he or she couldn't say no, regardless of the price, and provided preponderance of proof that the bargain was real. So, there is **the**

Secret Magic Formula . . .

In just seven words: prove you offer money at a discount.

secret magic formula, in just seven words: prove you offer money at a discount.

There are numerous consultants in the fields of real estate mortgages, office leases, utility bill auditing, and freight cost reduction who guarantee to help clients save at least $10,000.00, and require fees of only $1,000.00 to $2,000.00 or a percentage of monies saved. Well, who wouldn't agree to that deal?

That's the kind of money-at-a-discount "picture" you somehow have to engineer and present for your product or service. The same basic principle applies to negotiating other types of financial transactions. Again, you can sell just about anything if you can show the buyer how the thing (not the buyer) pays for the purchase, how the thing is, in effect, free.

Dan Kennedy's #8 No B.S. Truth About Selling

In persuading others to part with their money, your best possible approach is demonstrating that the apparent expense is not an actual expense at all; that the thing being purchased is either free or, better yet, actually pays.

You may never come across a situation where that demonstration is as clear-cut as it was with my client in the theft control business. I know I haven't come across another such situation. But the technique can be applied, to some degree, to most businesses. It may take some long, hard thought, some research, and some patience, but I assure you it's worth all that and more.

Sometimes this has a great deal to do with who you choose to sell to, and, although I'm going to cover the subject of prospecting later in this book, this is a good place to point out the impact of "The Who Factor" in your income and success in selling. **In many cases, the single most important factor governing a sales professional's income is who he chooses to sell to.** Not what he is selling, not its virtues and weaknesses, not its price, not competition, not his own sales skill level. Who he chooses to sell to. Stubborn marketers and sales professionals refuse to acknowledge how much "The Who Factor" matters, instead striving for improvement that is fundamentally unavailable from better propositions, better presentations, better skills, or greater effort.

Going back to my theft expert, there was a "sweet spot" for him, in the grocery store industry, once his fees topped $15,000.00. A single owner of one or even two neighborhood stores was not a good prospect; he had the problem, but the entire amount of inventory in the stores and his sales volume was too small. A big corporation with 30, 40, 50 stores was not ideal, because he had to sell to salaried executives who weren't having their own money stolen. The entrepreneurial owner of 4 to 12 stores—ideal.

Consider something like private air travel, whether charter or fractional jet ownership. It is so costly there's no possible money-at-a-discount argument to be made, *to most businesspeople.* I fly private, and to fly, say, from one of our homes near Cleveland to Orlando and, the next day or days later, back can cost $15,000.00 by private jet. To fly first class on Continental, no more than $1,500.00, or $3,000.00 if Carla and I are both traveling. Sure, flying private, you get free valet parking for your car and don't have to buy magazines at the airport, but c'mon. One of the very few types of people this can be sold to with a money-at-discount story is the person whose time has enormously high value, in terms of billable hours or deal-making. In private practice, for example, cosmetic surgeons and cosmetic dentists call it "chairside value." So a client of mine, a dentist, who has case values from $40,000.00 to $100,000.00+, and will chalk up about $20,000.00 for every day chairside, and has more patients on a waiting list than he can accept, sacrifices $20,000.00 for every day he's away. If he goes to speak at a seminar and loses a day going, a day there, and a day flying back, he's out of pocket $60,000.00. So if he flies there by private jet in the morning, speaks, and flies home that same afternoon, he "makes" $40,000.00. I'm in roughly the same position: my time at home, meeting with clients, or writing is worth, on average, about $30,000.00 a day. If I can buy a day for less than that with private jet travel vs. commercial flight, I'm buying money at a discount. Of course, I also have to be the sort of person who really *wants* to travel this way before it can be sold to me, but then the money-at-discount rationale helps a lot.

There's a similar, multifaceted profile to be identified for the ideal prospect for any product or service at any price point, and your income and enjoyment from selling will rise dramatically the more time you spend selling only to your ideal prospects.

How to Put Money in Their Pockets and Then Set It on Fire

You've undoubtedly heard the saying "his money's burning a hole in his pocket." It's used to describe people who can't keep their hands off their money; they can't wait to spend it. This is why furniture and electronic stores, auto dealerships and other

businesses bring in tax preparers and offer free tax return preparation and instant refunds during tax season—that refund is
instantly money burning a hole in the customer's pocket, and
he's quite likely to put out the fire before he gets out of the store!
I've done a lot of selling by first putting money in the prospect's
pocket, then setting it on fire. You can too. Let me explain.

When I sold millions of dollars of audio learning systems to
doctors in evening seminars, the seminars were free but the doctors had to post a $25.00 deposit to guarantee they would show
up; the deposit was "refundable" at the end of the seminar. After
presenting the "commercial" and closing the sale, I'd do a
"Columbo"—a sales technique named after the rumpled raincoat
character played by Peter Falk, famous for saying, "Just one more
thing . . . "—I would say, "Oh, just one more thing. You'll recall
you paid a $25.00 deposit to guarantee you'd be here this evening,
and you've kept that promise, so your $25.00 *is* refundable. And
we'll double that refund right before your very eyes; we'll match
it with $25.00 of our money, so you can deduct $50.00 from your
System purchase this evening. Just cross out the $499.00 price,
deduct the $50.00, and write $449.00 on your form."

Even with an audience that many would argue was too
sophisticated for such a strategy, this worked magically. What I
did was put $50.00 into their pockets and then set it on fire. If
they didn't buy a System, they "lost" that $50.00, and that hurt!
Learning from that, I've used "purchase roll-up" in countless
structured selling situations since. That means that the amount
you just spent for "x" is fully credited toward "y" if you act by
the deadline. In my own practice, for years, the initial day's consulting fee was credited and deducted from the much larger project fee if the client signed on then and there, which gave me a
near 100% "first call close" on sales from $50,000.00 to
$500,000.00.

The idea is simple: if they fail to buy or to upgrade, they
"lose" money already invested or already in their pocket.

Creating this "loss" changes the entire perception of price, and moves the prospect from thinking about what he's spending to what he's about to lose by failing to act.

I've replicated this strategy in other group sales situations in person-to-person selling, even in direct-mail campaigns. In fact, all discounts or bonuses tied to deadline dates in direct marketing offers live this strategy.

Becoming an "Added-Value" Sales Professional

Many sales professionals feel challenged by commoditization, and in some fields price shopping facilitated by the internet has worsened the situation, or at least their own perception of the situation.

A handful of years ago, I spoke at the Advertising Specialty Institute's national convention, where all the people who sell imprinted giveaway items like pens, litter bags, snow scrapers, key chains, etc. congregate. I opened my talk with this statement:

"If you are in a commodity business, get out."

Afterward, I got a lengthy, outraged letter from one attendee who accused me of being a lazy idiot who hadn't bothered to gain any understanding of their business and had insulted them by telling them to get out of business.

She missed the point.

Others in the room and in that industry who I work with got the point: that their business is commoditized, that the "trinkets" can be easily price-shopped, and that to prosper, they must focus on bringing "added value" to clients. To counter this, some have designed year-long, multistep, multimonth customer retention and reward programs for businesses involving the delivery of one of these same ad specialty products every month. Others have customized "trinket" based promotions for certain industries—like the Mother's Day cultured pearl promotion built for a restaurant owners. The pearls are a generic premium available to any one, and can be price shopped, but the pearls "bundled" with a turn-key, ready to use promotion including Mother's Day cards, postcards, coupons, window signs, table tents, even a website cannot be easily price-shopped. The added value makes the sale possible, and at premium prices to boot.

One of our Members, Nigel Worrall of Leisure Vacation Homes, manages and makes available homes in Orlando, Florida, for vacation rental, and in that business, he's up against price competition all over the internet. But with the added value of membership in his vacation club, arranged adventures—from backstage Disney tours to private astronaut training to race car driving adventures, and many other extra services—he doesn't simply set himself apart from competition, he changes the entire conversation and places his company in a category of one. I also mention him here because he has entered the premium business I just mentioned one paragraph above, by "packaging" vacation home rentals and selling them to businesses to use as gifts-with-purchase premiums or other sales incentives. The page from the customer newsletter put out by another of our Members, Diana Couto of Diana's Gourmet Pizzeria, features a vacation package from Nigel as a giveaway. (See Figure 10.1.)

Not long ago, I bought a classic car from a seller in Florida. I needed to get it moved by a transport company to Ohio, checked

Nigel's Selling Strategies

Get a look at Nigel's selling strategies at FloridaLeisure.com, MyDreamsComeTrue.com, and at FriendsDon'tLetFriends StayInHotels.com.

out by a good mechanic, whatever work needed, done. I needed to get the title changed and get its license plates. The auto shop that got my business—run by another of our Members who understands how to sell, Keith McCrone of Automotive Specialty Services—took care of arranging for the transport and receiving the car so I wasn't bothered with talking to transporters and juggling my own schedule to take delivery of the car; using my power of attorney to get the title changed and get the plates; inspected the car, faxed me the list of needed work for my okay; temporarily garaged the car; and delivered the car to me by appointment at my convenience. The added value here is maximum convenience—minimum hassle, a great way to add value to many things, especially if selling to affluent or busy clients.

These are the questions of the day: how can you add value to your core deliverables, so as to . . . create competitive differentiation, even create your own category of one . . . escape commoditization and price-based comparison shopping . . . and make yourself more appealing to certain clients, even if customizing the "package" of core and value added services for the individual client?

In simple terms, stop trying to sell what you've got and start selling what customers want and can't get—at least all under one roof—anywhere else.

Be Able To Say: No Other _____ Will . . .

The New Economy can be most succinctly summarized as: more demanding. More demanding of what? Of many things. Of *everything*. But above all other things, more demanding of the *truly* unique benefit. Sales professionals who insist on selling the same products and services without adding a truly unique benefit obtainable only by their customers will find The New Economy a difficult economy.

The response from most sales professionals will be: "But, there's nothing unique about what I sell." Well, whining about that won't fix it, will it? A key word in the last sentence of the above paragraph: *adding*.

One of my Members is a very successful financial advisor who targets only owners of businesses with $5 to $15 million of investable assets, and family succession issues within their businesses. He hosts quarterly three-day mastermind meetings exclusively for his clients, where he brings in top attorneys, psychologists, authors, and experts in family businesses. He says to his clients: "No other financial advisor will bring you together with 50 to 100 other family business owners in similar financial

"*How much would you pay for all the secrets of the universe? Wait, don't answer yet. You also get this six-quart covered combination spaghetti pot and clam steamer. Now how much would you pay?*"

situations, to network, share ideas, advise each other, even identify profitable strategic alliance opportunities." The key words
there are "no other financial advisor will".

Creating Added Value from Thin Air

When I sell my audio learning systems that have to do with
advertising and marketing, as well as Glazer-Kennedy Insider's
Circle™ Memberships, I often include "critique coupons" that
entitle the person to send me their ads, brochures, or sales letters
for analysis of what they've done effectively and what could be
done better. This is called a "second opinion consultation," for
which I usually charge from several hundred to several thousand
dollars, depending on the complexity of the piece being
reviewed. It is easy to make the case that each of these coupons
has a minimum value of $100.00. With a learning system that I
sell at many seminars for $278.00, I might include three coupons,
so the customer gets $300.00 of added value with a $278.00 purchase. (A voided sample of such a coupon is shown at the end of
this chapter, Figure 10.2. It cannot be used and is here for example purposes only.)

Interestingly, many sales professionals give away certain
services that have real value, but that they do not quantify and
present as added value. Others err in giving away "unlimited"
service, which can't then be quantified and value. If I tell you that
you can send in material anytime all year as often as you like for
critique, that has no value, because you don't know how much
you'll use and it is vague. But if I give you three $100.00-value
service certificates, we can agree on that as $300.00 of value.
Ironically, the three is a more limited offer than the open-ended,
yet in selling, it is more persuasive.

Many sales pros have more than one opportunity to add to
the value argument by formalizing, quantifying, and placing values on services they routinely include.

Creating Added Value at Nominal Cost

One of the best benefits provided by the internet is unlimited "library space" at virtually zero cost. Gold and Diamond Level Glazer-Kennedy Insider's Circle™ Members have access codes for different restricted-access websites, each inventoried with different archives including past issues of the *NO B.S. MARKETING LETTER* and other newsletters, transcripts of my interviews with top advertising, marketing, and sales experts, articles, a different "encore" audio program each month, and other resources, many with a searchable index, as well as online communities for networking with other Members. This expands and grows more valuable every month. It is significant added value to Members, yet costs nearly nothing to provide.

Many businesses can and do use this idea. In my Membership, that I know of, there are attorneys, CPAs, chiropractors, ad specialty salespeople, insurance sales professionals, brokers, a manufacturer supplying the pharmaceutical industry, and dozens of others, each providing useful collections of information only to their customers through restricted access websites.

You can also create added value through premiums, guarantees and warranties, special services, frequent-user rebates, club

GKIC Membership

To get a closer look at how we provide added value to our Members, why not take advantage of my invitation to two FREE months of Gold Membership? You'll receive newsletters, webinars, and other resources free, and you can try out the online resources shared by Gold Members. To get started immediately, visit www.FreeGiftFrom.com.sales.

memberships—turn your imagination loose and find an opportunity that matches your particular business. Added value allows you to make your "core" goods or services "free."

FIGURE 10.1: Diana Couto's Gourmet Pizzeria Newsletter Page

FIGURE 10.2: Critique Certificate

$100.00 Critique Certificate $100.00

Entitles bearer to submit any single printed piece;
brochure; catalog; direct-mail piece; advertisement or similar
promotional material by mail for critique by Dan S. Kennedy.

Send Certificate and Materials to:

Dan S. Kennedy

Glazer-Kennedy Insider's Circle™

402 Jefferson Ave.

Towson, MD 21286

Terms and Conditions

Certificate expires 12 months from date of purchase. Allow 4 to 6 weeks
for Mr. Kennedy's response. Do NOT telephone; consultation given by
mail only. Actual finished materials or "rough sketch" and copy for
planned material may be submitted. Coupon redeemable only for listed
services. Additional consulting may be contracted for, Mr. Kennedy's
schedule permitting; fees quoted on request.

Please be advised that any materials submitted for review by Dan
Kennedy, including those submitted with critique coupons, may be published in any of Dan Kennedy authored/edited publications, as examples. Also, submitted materials will not be returned. Do not submit
materials you are concerned about keeping confidential.

CHAPTER 11

STRATEGY 11
ALWAYS COMPARE
APPLES TO ORANGES

"**Y**ou can't compare apples to oranges."

I'm sure you've heard that; I encourage you to get it completely out of your mind! The secret to eliminating price resistance *is* to compare apples to oranges! Let me give you a personal example:

During one four-year period, I built the largest integrated publishing and seminar business exclusively serving chiropractors and dentists in North America. In my seminars for SuccessTrak Inc., I sold a 12-month "trak" (subscription) of audio programs on practice promotion and success subjects. Counting the bonus items, there were 18 audio programs in the one-year program—sold then for $499.00.

At the time, most audio programs, available on a variety of topics, sold for an average of $10.00 each. On that basis, these 18 audio programs would have sold for only $180.00. My price was 275% above par. The economics of marketing via free seminars required that we sell for the considerably higher price. Also, due to the specialized, valuable nature of the information in these programs, we felt justified in commanding the higher price. But how do you clearly and successfully justify that price to the consumer? Obviously, if you compare other apples to apples, the commodity to the commodity, you're dead.

In this case, we compared audio programs to seminars. If the participants obtained the same basic information that was in the audio programs by attending the seminars on which they were based, the doctors would have spent thousands of dollars on enrollment fees alone, not to mention time away from their practices during the week (which is very costly) or away from family on weekends, travel and lodging costs, and other expenses. All things considered, by buying the audio programs, people could save much more than $3,000.00!

By switching to an apples-to-oranges comparison, I presented a compelling argument of savings to the consumer. (This also relates to Strategy 10: Sell Money at a Discount.)

In Figure 11.1, you'll find a "Big Lesson of the Month" reprinted from an issue of my *No B.S. Marketing Letter,* this one titled: Rig the Game. It includes another illustration of apples to oranges.

Most of the Advice You Get About Dealing with Price Resistance Is Wrong

If you deal with price resistance by arguing in favor of your higher quality, your better service, etc., you will find your sales work difficult most of the time. People do want superior quality goods and services, but they still don't enjoy paying premium prices for them. Many marketers fight that battle unnecessarily.

It is much easier and much more effective to switch the standards of comparison. Win by comparing apples to oranges and then "throw in" the superior quality at "no extra cost."

If you are in a selling situation where there is heads-on competition, even competitive bidding, this technique can still be used. There was a situation in which I was consulting with a manufacturing company in direct competitive bid warfare with a lower-price opponent, losing bid after bid. I said: "Something has to change here." They said: "It can't. We can't cut our prices any lower." I said: "If we can't come in with the lower bid, we might as well come in with an even higher bid—but let's change the rules of the game when we do it." They began changing the specifications for the bids, adding value, bundling goods and services together, extending warranties and including delivery and completion guarantees. Then we built a "HOW TO COMPARE OUR BID WITH OTHERS" Checklist. When it was all said and done, they started getting projects they'd been losing to low bidders before.

The savvy sales pro learns to alter the "rules of the games" to give himself or herself an overwhelming advantage. Forget all about "playing fair." Forget all about competing on a "level playing field." These are clichés that are best lasered out of your consciousness. All your life, you've been told to "play fair," and that conditioning of your subconscious may be holding you back now. Selling in competitive situations is all about finding or inventing an *unfair* advantage for yourself.

That's exactly the approach I took with this client. I analyzed their operations and discovered that they were in a position to include warehousing and fulfillment at a much lower cost than their competitor could possibly do. By adding that service to their specifications, their higher quote became the most attractive quote.

Specialization and Customization Prevent Apples to Apples Comparisons

In one of the issues of my *No B.S. Marketing Letter*, I featured the ads of a company selling a nutritional supplement to improve eyesight, labeled for and advertised in magazines read by hunters. Unbeknownst to those reading the magazines for outdoorsmen, the same company advertised the same product, labeled differently, in magazines for private pilots. In truth, the nutrients with potential of improving eyesight are limited, and eyesight improvement is eyesight improvement, so you could buy these exact same supplements from any health food store shelf for significantly less money. But the fact that this product was for a very particular customer precludes price shopping by most, and the fact that it's being advertised and sold in specialized media read only by those particular customers creates a competition and comparison free zone in which to make the sale. The exact same principles apply to selling in person, face to face, to customers or clients; consumers or B2B. You want to be perceived and presented as a specialist for a particular type of customer, with products or services specifically for them, and you want to use that positioning to create a competition and comparison free zone to sell in. For more depth on this, I urge reading Chapters 36 and 37 of my book, *No B.S. Marketing to the Affluent.*

In concert, the strategy of customization. To stay in the same product category, if I decide on a vitamin, mineral, and herbal supplement regimen by myself and go to the health food store, a catalog, or a website to buy products, I'll have some pre-conceived thoughts about what I might be willing to spend—and if one of the products I want is Omega-3 Fish Oil, I may very well price shop it or otherwise compare one brand to another, and weigh its source, potency, and price. But if I go to my doctor and get a battery of blood tests, hair analysis and other assessments, then a personal prescription for exactly what I need to take, specifying the precise number of milligrams of this and ounces of that, and that exact product combination is then offered to me by that doctor, will I take the list of components and ingredients and go search for different, cheaper alternatives to assemble my own package? 99% won't. They will not question or consider price at all. They will take the prescription. Why? Three reasons—and you want to replicate all three in your own selling:

1. The prescription came from an authority figure, not perceived as "a salesman."
2. The customer sought out the expert and his advice including his specific prescription.
3. The seller provided a customized, personalized product.

If you'd like to permanently escape the world of apples to apples comparisons, there's *your* prescription.

FIGURE 11.1: Excerpt from *No B.S. Marketing Lesson*, BIG Lesson, 1/07

"Rig the Game"

If you've ever been down the midway of a county fair, state fair, or traveling carnival, you've undoubtedly forked over money to either not win a prize or get a $2 stuffed animal for $38…playing some game that looks ridiculously easy. Knock over big, lunky metal milk bottles with a softball. (Softballs rigged to slow in mid-air, bottles weighted at bottom.) Toss a penny into any one of a zillion fish bowls filled with water. (Bowls are so close together, bowl lips curve in . . . pennies hit and bounce off.) Etc. the games are all rigged. In Vegas, they actually tell everybody the games are rigged—bragging that their slots return 97% of the money pumped into them and not one penny more. (The lure there—even with knowledge certain that everybody loses, you might win. But the house never loses.) Bob Stupak, who I got to know a little, who built Vegas World from a one floor slots-only dump to giant "last hotel on The Strip," now the Stratosphere (with direct marketing and publicity stunts) hired M.I.T. wizards to create Vegas games that

FIGURE 11.1: Excerpt from *No B.S. Marketing Lesson,*
BIG Lesson, 1/07, continued

looked easier to win—like "crapless craps," with every number a point number, and blackjack with the dealer's cards face up . . . but these games were otherwise rigged so their percentage favored the house even more than the regular games! In the entire world of "games of chance," the owners of the games never take a chance at all. They rig every game in their favor. (Big Lesson #1 of the New Year.)

Advertising, marketing, sales all have profound similarities to presenting games of chance; similarities too numerous and complex for this page. The similarities demand that you, the marketer, rig the game. One game-rigging technique I teach everywhere—from my *No B.S. Sales Success* book on up—is "apples to oranges, never apples to apples" comparisons. You control the comparative judgment made by the prospect. You do NOT leave it up to the prospect or to other marketers to choose comparisons to be made. (Big Lesson #2.)

Shown here, a very successful use of this technique by long-time Member Paul Johnston, owner of The Shed Shop, a builder of backyard sheds sold at VERY premium prices, at three-times to six-times what you can buy a backyard shed for at Lowes, HomeDepot, or from other shed companies that advertise heavily in his markets. **How do you sell at prices 300% to 600% higher than very visible competitors advertising cheaper prices?** Rig the game. ONLY by rigging the game. In his case, his first breakthrough came by switching from talking about sheds (construction, quality, blah, blah, blah) to talking about customers' stories and their uses of the sheds, enjoyment, pride of ownership. But the second big breakthrough is shown here—NOT comparing shed to shed, but comparing shed to remodeling and a room addition. If you are a critical thinker and saw "backyard shed," "rented storage

FIGURE 11.1: Excerpt from *No B.S. Marketing Lesson,*
BIG Lesson, 1/07, continued

shed," "small trailer," and "room addition" on an IQ test, and had to toss the one that doesn't belong, you'd eliminate "room addition." On its face, comparing a shed to a room addition is like comparing a car to a jet airplane, and pointing out how much less it costs to own the car. Ridiculous. Fortunately, selling and critical thinking by buyers are just as divorced. (Big Lesson #3.)

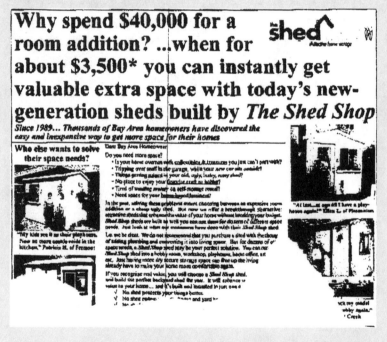

Here's the top part of one of the Shed Shop ads, with the game-rigging comparison. Incidentally, if you were on the December Gold Call, you heard "Lieutenant X" describe his brilliant use of this exact same strategy to get $78.00 a month for a product, in an environment where many competitors are all advertising a "standard," normal, and customary price of $28.00. That's a

FIGURE 11.1: Excerpt from *No B.S. Marketing Lesson,*
  BIG Lesson, 1/07, continued

280% multiple. It means needing only 1,282 customers to make each $100,000.00 per month desired, vs. needing 3,571 customers . . . if, say, it cost $150.00 to acquire a customer, it would require $192,300.00 in invested capital to create the $1.2-million business rather than $535,650.00, which might permit creating it much faster. Retention of customers can be much, much better because the better margin affords doing more for them. And on and on. The benefits of selling at higher prices/higher margins than everyone else vying for your customers' attention and loyalty are many. One of the best strategies for doing so is "apples/oranges, never apples/apples." Mmmmm, tasty.

CHAPTER 12

STRATEGY 12
IN SEARCH OF
THE FREE LUNCH

There's an old story about the king who commissioned a group of the brightest scholars in his kingdom to assemble the wisdom of the ages. They first came back with a truckload full of stone tablets. He told them to condense and simplify. They came with an encyclopedia. He demanded that they condense and simplify. Finally, ultimately, they returned with a single sentence: there's no such thing as a free lunch.

Every sane, sensible logical person knows that to be the truth. However, we all still love to believe there might be! That's why premiums work so well in selling. A premium is a free gift or a free bonus: something the buyer gets free when purchasing something else. Everything from books to Buicks have been given away at one time or another as a premium with a purchase.

Every single time you hear "free," logic says it's a lie. If you hear it from an advertiser, marketer, or salesperson, it's a lie. If you hear it from a politician, it's an even bigger lie. Yet it's still a very sweet and seductive thing to hear. Politicians keep right on giving Huey Long's "chicken in every pot, car in every garage" speech, and it actually seems to be more and more effective with each election. The gift-with-purchase gambit credited by most as invention by Estee Lauder continues to be a staple not just in the cosmetics field, but just about everywhere. Some people actually believe they get free drinks in casinos!

I personally love to use premiums in selling. I've given away cameras, vacation trips, books, reports, subscriptions, collectors' art prints, free consulting services, jewelry, and many other things in personal, group, and mail-order selling over the years. Here are some tips on using premiums:

- Don't give away the same things you sell. In most cases, this is a bad practice because it devalues your merchandise or services.
- Offer premiums that people want for themselves. Even if you're in the business-to-business marketing environment, it's best to offer a luxury personal-use item, at least as one of two or more options.
- Give away things people want but rarely buy for themselves. I've found that people will often buy something as a premium that they ordinarily would never buy on its own. A day at the spa is a compelling premium when selling to women who do not ordinarily buy such an indulgence for themselves.
- Make the premium relevant to your offer or to your customers or clients. It doesn't have to necessarily be related to what you are selling. It can be. But it can be relevant to your customers yet unrelated to your product or service.

How to Close the Difficult Sale
with a Very Desirable Premium

For many years, the direct selling companies in the home security and fire alarm systems businesses have relied on desirable
premiums. Although everybody needs and should have a fire
alarm system in their home, nobody wants one, and so it is a
difficult sale. Typically, these companies will offer a beautiful
set of crystal and dinnerware, or a gorgeous collection of jewelry,
or an all-expenses-paid vacation as the free bonus gift to close
the sale. This lets the buyers get something they really *want*
while doing the right thing and purchasing something they
really *need.* The gift may very well be something they would
never buy for themselves, but they love the opportunity of getting it "free."

Premiums and "Big Ticket Selling"

You can even use premiums in negotiating. With one big consulting contract I closed, I "threw in" a complete library of my books
and audio learning programs. The retail value was well over
$2,500.00, but the cost to me was less than $300.00. I once gave
away a certain amount of consulting time to an individual, for
his business, as a "bonus" for his investing in one of my companies. In selling a business, I included consulting time as a bonus.
I know a businessman who secured the services of a top lawyer
by including free use of a private plane in the agreement in addition to the normal retainers and fees.

A Member of mine, a commercial mortgage broker dealing
only with commercial real estate agents handling large apartment building transactions, periodically gives away a Palm
Springs golf resort vacation to the broker bringing him the most
business—highlighting this in his direct-mail has brought many
new brokers to him.

In the recent recession, one California builder of luxury beachfront homes began giving away one of his downtown condos as a free bonus with purchase of a home.

Another client of mine provides investment-related services to affluent M.D.s and surgeons. His "new client welcome gift" is a week's stay in the luxury beachfront condominium he owns in the Bahamas. He vacations there himself four weeks a year, leaving forty-eight weeks to give away to new clients.

You can use the "free-lunch technique" many different ways in business. Do not make the mistake of overlooking or discounting how powerful and universal the appeal of this approach is. Do not make the mistake of thinking it does not apply to high-priced products, professional services, or complex negotiations, or to sophisticated buyers or investors.

CHAPTER 13

STRATEGY 13
THE MAGIC OF MYSTIQUE

Part of the value of what someone does lies in how difficult others think it is to do. For example, in America, people say that public speaking is their number one fear. Incredibly, more people are afraid of speaking in public than of getting cancer, having a prolonged illness, or even dying! To me, however, public speaking has become just about the easiest thing I know how to do. I know, though, that I command a significant amount of respect from a group before I even speak a word, just by virtue of doing what they feel is so terrifyingly difficult to do. It is much, much harder to speak to a group of other professional speakers because to them there is no mystique in the speaking.

People wouldn't pay to see a magician perform if they knew exactly how the magic tricks were done. Remove the mystique and there's no product left. And that's true of most things. In sales and marketing it's important to create and preserve some mystique, glamour, intrigue, and uniqueness.

Perception Is Reality:
The "Story" Is the "Secret Ingredient"

McDonald's special sauce. The formula for Coca-Cola. Colonel Sander's secret recipe for KFC. These things preserve some mystique in otherwise mundane products.

Nowhere is this more visibly at work than in the cosmetics and skin-care products field, where I've done a lot of work as an advertising copywriter, with infomercials, with both private label products and retail salons. If you haven't paid much attention to this business, the next time you're at a department store, stroll slowly past the cosmetic counters. You will be astounded at how many different brand names, colors, scents, and mystifying products there are. The ingredients are incredible: dew collected only from tulips growing on the sunny side of the Swiss Alps, volcanic ash, seaweed from an exotic locale, even sheep sperm!

Yet, as much as the consumers of these products hate hearing this, all of it is pretty much the same. In fact, there's only one manufacturer for every 50 to 100 different brands, labels, and product lines—all with the same ingredients, the only significant differences being the packaging, price, and "story."

If you took away the mystique created by the stories, the celebrities, and the advertising, you'd have one generic line of cosmetics, warranting price points 50% to 500% less than today's going rates. But nobody would buy it, and everybody would hate you for revealing how the magician did the trick.

Creating Your Own Mystique

Developing mystique is possible for anyone. One technique is what I call "Takeaway Selling," which is explored in detail in

Part V of this book. Learning to use Takeaway Selling has had greater impact on my personal earnings than any other single thing I've ever discovered or learned, so be sure to study this section of the book. You'll find that some of the ideas regarded as "gospel" about success in selling are challenged.

Another "trick" is to create your own mystique terminology for what you do, just as the cosmetic manufacturers do. In the self-improvement industry, the all-time bestselling books *Psycho-Cybernetics* and *The New Psycho-Cybernetics* utilize language borrowed from missile guidance technology and robotics to describe human psychology and behavior, and use created, proprietary terminology like ASM, Automatic Success Conditioning and Theater of the Mind to organize and present information about fairly universal self-help activities, such as visualization. The once hugely successful and famous EST program built mystique around its unique language and terminology. In EST, you only knew if you had "it" when you got "it" and otherwise you couldn't understand what "it" was. EST's Werner Erhard learned this mystique-creating tactic from his earlier experiences in Mind Dynamics, the human potential seminar arm of the controversial cosmetic sales/pyramid marketing company, Holiday Magic. At introductory seminars for such programs, those already "in" would be talking enthusiastically and happily with one another in a language largely incomprehensible by the new guests. Because "outsiders" are naturally motivated to become "insiders," this situation alone helped sell these programs.

In my own development of and teaching of advertising, marketing, and selling strategies, I've coined a great deal of unique terminology, such as Message-To-Market Match, Shock and Awe Packages, Marketing By Values, 3-Step Letter System, and many, many more, for the express purpose of making concepts mine, and adding mystique. Clients in every imaginable field have followed suit: carpet cleaners, dentists, real estate agents, real estate trainers, financial advisors have all learned from me to name their concepts and processes, illustrate their concepts and processes, in some cases actually trademark their terminology, and use it all to convey an air of mystique, to proffer *secrets*.

One of the things I've learned in marketing as wide and diverse a variety of products and services as I have is that **"I've got a secret" is one of the most powerful of all positioning statements**. People at all levels, CEO to broom-pusher, desperately want to believe in secrets—that there is some piece of information that has been kept from them, that others know but they do not, that will resolve their biggest problem or fulfill their greatest desire. If you can reposition yourself as a seller of secrets, you instantly gain power.

How to Unmask and Still Create Mystique

More than 18 years ago, I wrote a book, *The Ultimate Sales Letter*, which is still available in bookstores in an up-dated edition, in which I reveal and demonstrate each of the 28 steps that I go through as a professional direct-response copywriter to create powerful sales letters or ads for my clients—at fees starting at $50,000.00 up plus royalties. I revealed every step I take, but still, many people read the book and choose to hire me anyway. Why? Because there's enough intangible creativity and mystique in what I do that even when you know the steps of the process, you may not be able to do it as well as I can. Also, the very fact that I have a systematic, proprietary process influences many clients. This is an example of how you can reveal what's behind your curtain yet still have people more convinced they should hire you to do it for them than to do it themselves.

A number of years back, I watched Chuck Daly and Brendan Suhr conduct a practice and a coaching session with the Detroit Pistons, and then coach a big game. I'm a quick learner, so I think I understand the structure of what they did and why they did it. But I still couldn't duplicate their experience and talent at applying the process. In fact, I left with a greater appreciation for what they do than I had before. And were I to own an NBA team, I wouldn't be so foolish as to take its head coach role. I'd find and hire the best.

If what you do creates that kind of awe and respect, then you can create mystique by revealing your process rather than concealing it. If what you do doesn't create awe and respect, you ought to go to work fixing that!

Everything Old Is New Again—at Least It Better Be!

One related matter that messes up a lot of people in marketing is "what's new?" A sales rep in one of our companies was once overheard complaining that we hadn't introduced any new products for a long time. "Have all your customers seen all of our products?" I asked. The rep freely admitted they had not. "Then you've got new products," I said.

A funny thing occasionally happens in the advertising business: a client will cancel or change an ad campaign that's working perfectly just because they got bored with it and assumed everybody else was, too. That's a bad assumption. There are ad campaigns that sustain success for five, even ten years. These campaigns are old hat to their owners but are new to new customers who are paying attention to them for the first time. If it's unknown to someone, it's a secret—regardless of how routine it may be to you.

I had to learn that in my consulting activities. I charge fees for disclosing knowledge that to me is quite ordinary. To those who need to know it and don't, it's exotic and valuable. For example, I know quite a bit about how to select and obtain mailing lists for just about any purpose. If you need a list of middle-aged dog owners who live in Philadelphia, subscribe to *Better Homes and Gardens,* and have at least one credit card, I know how to get that list. To me, there's nothing to that. To those who don't know and need to, it's worth a lot, and is quite mystifying and impressive.

The New Economy doesn't demand everything successfully sold in it *actually* be new. In fact, many New Economy Customers are more sensitive than ever to "proven." Trustworthiness and reliability matter. However, whatever you sell needs to be presented in a way that feels timely and current and, to some audience "hip," to some customers "cutting edge." Customers want innovation, they just don't want to be guinea pigs and lab rats.

You cannot permit yourself to lose interest in or enthusiasm for your most tried and true products and services that have proven themselves appealing, satisfying, and valuable to customers. But you do need to freshen the presentation of such things frequently. In truth, hardly any product, service, person, place, or thing has inherent mystique. Paris, France, is no more inherently interesting than Paris, Kentucky, absent its romantic reputation, image, story. If you feel deprived by not having something to sell with mystique and, worse, waste energy looking for such a thing, you need to change your thinking about this and accept the responsibility of the masterfully persuasive sales professional—to provide the mystique.

CHAPTER 14

STRATEGY 14
I'D RATHER BE DUMB AND PERSISTENT THAN SMART AND IMPATIENT

A friend of mine tells a story about a dumb frog that fell into a big barrel half full of cream. He was close to drowning, and all the other frogs circled the top of the barrel and laughed and jeered at him. But this frog was so dumb he thought they were cheering him on, so he paddled faster and faster and faster until he churned the cream into butter, and then he was able to hop back out of the barrel.

It's possible to be too smart, to know so much that you know all the reasons why it won't, can't, and shouldn't work. While you are sitting around stymied by all those problems, some dumb frog down the road is doing it!

Now, with all my experience, I have to continually fight the disadvantage of being "too smart." Yes, it can be a disadvantage.

You can be too familiar with what has not worked in the past, thus too close-minded to new ideas or re-testing old ones under new conditions.

How Being a Dumb Frog Got This
Rookie a Veteran's Top Income—Fast

I remember at the very beginning of my speaking career getting cornered at a National Speakers Association workshop by a very successful, very prominent "old pro." He generously explained to me, at great length and in great detail, all "the dues" I would have to pay to "get good" before I could even hope to do well in the business. He painted a rather dreary picture of years of begging for low-paid or even zero-compensation opportunities to speak and gain exposure. He told me that if I made a practice of hanging around guys like him and watching their every move, I might amount to something some day.

Finally, when I could get a word in edgewise, I brought up the subject of money. Instead of talking about the number of different audiences he had spoken to or the number of miles he had traveled, I wanted to hear about money: the only real measurement of the worth of a person, product, or service in the marketplace. I asked how much might I expect to earn in the business. His long-winded answer culminated with: ". . .as much as $100,000.00 a year after 10 or 15 years." I said: "Pardon me, but I made $5,000.00 my first month, and it looks like I'll top $100,000.00 this year, my first year. I was sort of looking for someone who was really doing a big job." I did, in fact, top $100,000.00 my first year and routinely made from $250,000.00 to $1-million most years thereafter.

I don't tell that story to be arrogant or to rub the other guy's nose in it, but rather to illustrate this point: this guy did know all the ropes. He really understood the business inside and out and upside down. Compared to him, I was a dumb frog. And I was going about some things the hard way. (For example, I was selling myself as a speaker door-to-door, business-to-business, in person.) But through ignorance, confidence, patience, and determination, I was getting spectacular results.

The next time you run into one of these know-it-all "experts" who gives you all the reasons you *can't* succeed, walk away. Who are they—who am I, for that matter—to tell you what *you* can't do? When I wrote the first edition of this book, there was a guy pitching in major league baseball with one arm. I wonder how many people tried "for his own good" to convince him to forget about baseball? The experts in the amusement park business laughed Walt Disney out of a meeting room. Among other things, they told him the idea of having just one entrance and exit for a big park was the dumbest idea of the century. I could fill a book with such stories, including quite a few of my own, times when different grizzled old pros and anointed experts have told me I couldn't do what I went right on and did.

Unfortunately, salespeople new to a particular selling environment are often set upon by these grizzled veterans—the resident experts in everything that's already been tried and everything that won't work. Often, their beliefs and biases haven't been tested in years, and are now erroneous. This is especially true in The New Economy. What was working may not work well now; what didn't work might be just the ticket. There's a lot to be said for finding out some things for yourself.

There's also something to be said—although cautiously—for persistence.

There was a time in my life when I put "persistence" on a much more exalted pedestal than I do now. In fact, I talked about it in the earlier editions of this book without caveat, which I have corrected here and now. There is a fine line between essential and admirable persistence and stubborn, costly stupidity. All astute entrepreneurs and marketers learn to welcome the swift sword. To find out what won't work as quickly and cheaply as possible, then on to the next experiment. In concert, though, if they find or figure out something that shows promise, they have bulldog tenacity and tremendous patience in tinkering, tweaking, testing, and tinkering some more, to get it fully functional. They are then very resistant to others' discouraging opinions. I would suggest these three **New Economy Rules:**

1. Be very open-minded to testing new, or, for that matter, old ideas and strategies under new conditions.
2. Be very quick to abandon those that show little or no promise, regardless of your hopes for them.
3. Be patient and persistent with those that do show promise, regardless of anybody else's opinions.

Even we legendary experts can be wrong! In my Platinum Inner Circle several years ago, one of its 18 Members, a marketing expert for the mortgage industry, announced a brand new, radical approach he was implementing, in selling subscriptions to his publications. I saw and enunciated three major drawbacks to his idea and concluded that it was fraught with more peril than it was worth. The other Members agreed. He ignored us all and tested his premise. Today we all use his strategy.

Does Success—or Failure—Breed Success?

In my speaking career of about 30 years, I've built 19 different platform selling presentations for my own use, culminating with the one I used at all the public seminars with Zig Ziglar and many other engagements for 10 very successful years. Each one has provided me with excellent income. Each one, however, started out as a failure. Each one produced unsatisfactory results the first few times I used it, but each of those times, I learned from the audience reactions what was working and what wasn't. Then I adjusted the presentation, delivered it again, observed and learned, adjusted again, until I finally "hit." Fortunately,

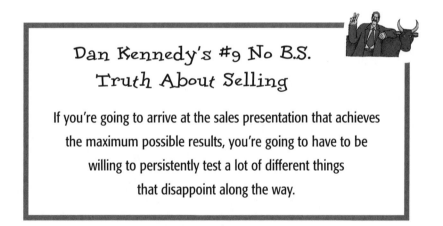

each successive one has required less of this, thanks to the cumulative experience. Still, it's the willingness to fail and the failure itself that makes success possible.

My friend Ted Nicholas, famous self-publisher and promoter of the best-selling book *How to Form Your Own Corporation without a Lawyer for Under $75.00,* has sold over $200-million worth of all of his books through mail-order ads he has written himself. Yet he'll cheerfully tell you that eight out of ten of his ads failed. It's what he learned from the failures that made it possible for him to create the big winners—direct-response ads that returned two, three, four, and even five times their ad cost consistently, month after month, year after year. This experience is shared by most direct marketers and direct-response advertisers, who are, essentially salespeople selling one-to-many by media rather than one-to-one by manual labor. It is certainly my experience.

Dan Kennedy's #9 No B.S. Truth About Selling

If you're going to arrive at the sales presentation that achieves the maximum possible results, you're going to have to be willing to persistently test a lot of different things that disappoint along the way.

Don't ever mistake genius for persistence. When you look at top achievers in any field, selling included, the temptation is to credit them with genius status, which makes it impossible for an ordinary mortal like yourself to match them. But the truth is, more often than not, their current ability to perform is the result of dogged persistence, methodical testing and tinkering, discarding what doesn't work, identifying what does, not gifted genius, and *that* you can replicate.

CHAPTER 15

STRATEGY 15
LONG DISTANCE IS NOWHERE NEAR AS GOOD AS BEING THERE

These days, a lot of companies have cut travel budgets, distance travel is so onerous that I have drastically altered the ways I do business, and e-mail, tele-conferencing, video-conferencing, text messaging, Twittering, etc. seems to have taken over the world's communication. There are, however, times and circumstances when nothing short of person-to-person, human contact will get the job done, and there are selling situations so lucrative or important that nothing short of that should be employed.

Given everyone's preference for the ease, convenience, low cost, and haste of impersonal, at-distance communication, I believe that New Economy Customers will be more persuasively influenced than ever before by the sales professional who invests himself in meeting with them in person. The willingness to get on your horse and ride over there is now an even more significant competitive advantage, but it's not new.

Some 30 years ago, a company I took over was in deep trouble with a primary, essential vendor. The company owed the vendor a huge sum of money, comprising due and past-due bills, some as old as 150 days. The vendor had shut off shipments. They would not even ship COD; they wanted payments on the old bills. The comptroller of our company had tried to work some practical arrangement out with the vendor, and several weeks of correspondence and telephone calls had been invested without any results.

I called the vendor and left word for the president that I was flying in to meet with him, would arrive the following morning, and would stay as long as necessary to resolve the problem in a mutually beneficial manner.

I flew to Minneapolis, rented a car, and drove to the vendor's plant. The president and I met for five hours. I let him vent his frustrations; I let him see that I was not equipped with horns, a tail, and a three-pronged pitchfork and I explained our situation. As the end of the meeting, I had our pending shipments released on an open account, a new open-account credit line sufficient for our needs, and the accumulated amounts due converted to a long-term installment note with no interest. I am absolutely convinced that this could never have been negotiated long distance. And I have never forgotten my comptroller's insistence that it was a waste of time and money, that he had already exhausted every option and negotiating ploy. He had. Except for face-to-face. I've never forgotten the lesson learned.

The late Mark McCormack, the famous sports agent with whom I appeared on several seminar programs, said: "I will often fly great distances to meet someone face-to-face, even when I can say much of what needs to be said over the phone." I believe this practice was fundamental to his exceptional success at securing and keeping the top athletes and sports personalities as his clients and for negotiating large numbers of lucrative deals for them. He was willing to do what most people are too lazy and too cheap to do: meet face-to-face. Note those words: lazy; cheap. I mean them. I have very recently seen great opportunities and potentially beneficial relationships slip away into the ether just because clients of mine ignored my advice and were too lazy and too cheap to charter a jet and fly in to a meeting. Millions lost to save a few thousand dollars and avoid a half-day of inconvenience. Of course, they would insist they are neither lazy nor cheap; that they are sensible; they are very busy with many responsibilities, so why go there when a tele-conference can do the job? Answer: because it can't.

I have negotiated solutions to huge legal disputes, arranged lines of credit under adverse circumstances, raised capital from private and commercial sources, sold large-fee consulting contracts, and otherwise experienced a lengthy list of notable sales and negotiation victories by doing whatever was necessary to get face-to-face with the other person or people involved. In selling a division of one of my companies to a competitor, I didn't bother with preliminary correspondence or a telephone conversation. I just called the company president and said, "I want to fly over and meet with you for an hour or so to present an idea I think you'll be interested in." By starting out face-to-face, I believe I ensured the success of the proposition and slashed weeks off the time required to create and close the deal.

There is no substitute for face-to-face, personal contact in selling. I *am* a big believer in substituting tools and other marketing methods for person-to-person contact work in prospecting, as I've described elsewhere in this book. I *detest* investing productive personal time in meetings with people who are not qualified or ready to do business. But, on the other hand, I very much prefer getting face-to-face with someone who is qualified and ready to do business. In fact, if the typical sales professional could switch from spending 80% of his time trying to get to opportunities to sell and only 20% of his time selling to the inverse—only 20% of his time trying to get there, 80% actually selling—he would increase his income four-fold or five-fold, with no other change, and no improvement in selling skill. And that is why Part II of this book may prove to be the single most important set of pages you ever read about your sales career!

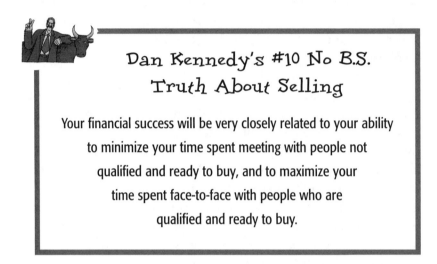

Dan Kennedy's #10 No B.S. Truth About Selling

Your financial success will be very closely related to your ability to minimize your time spent meeting with people not qualified and ready to buy, and to maximize your time spent face-to-face with people who are qualified and ready to buy.

PART II

HOW TO STOP PROSPECTING
ONCE AND FOR ALL

CHAPTER 16

POSITIONING, NOT PROSPECTING

I t has been my observation that the weakest link in the selling chain for most salespeople is prospecting. Most people can do at least an adequate job of presenting their products or services, if there's a reasonably interested prospect in front of them. But most of the salespeople I've encountered simply hate prospecting. Consequently, they avoid it, both consciously and unconsciously, and do it only when the dire necessity of imminent starvation pushes them to it, and then they do it poorly.

And do you know what? I hate prospecting too. If I had to acquire my clients, my speaking engagements, my consulting assignments, and my writing projects by prospecting, I'd be driving a cab for a living. To me, prospecting is grubby, unpleasant

"*Mr. Smith's office doesn't have a door. You have to batter your way through the wall.*"

work. To me, there's no worse way to spend time than talking to people who are not interested, are not qualified to say yes even if they were interested, and who view me as someone they have to defend themselves against.

I'm here to tell you: I do NOT think you should prospect. Especially now, in The New Economy, when potential customers and clients, by recession conditioning, step back and away from the sales professional coming toward them as if he were a drooling, rabies-infected, flea-infested dog—even when what he has to offer is of interest to them. Traditional prospecting is going to be less productive than ever, for the foreseeable future. Just being visibly engaged in traditional prospecting makes you glow toxic.

What you need to do is to focus on positioning. By that I mean *positioning yourself so that good, qualified prospects find out about you and seek you out to obtain your expert assistance in solving their problems...or at least feel they are finding you and seeking you out.*

Incidentally, it's perfectly okay to pursue them in follow-up, once they feel they've discovered you, made the first move toward you, and invited the communication. In fact, it's foolish and irresponsible not to follow-up. But that first move needs to be theirs.

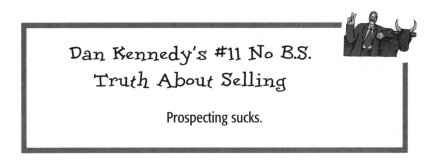

Dan Kennedy's #11 No B.S. Truth About Selling

Prospecting sucks.

Why is this so important? Because when you go to prospects and present yourself, their guard goes up. They perceive you as someone there to get something from them. This is when "sales resistance" sets in. But when somebody discovers you, and takes the initiative to seek you out for your expert assistance, then that person's guard is down. "Sales receptiveness" rules.

Here are some opportunities for prospects to discover you.

Writing

Writing and being published is a powerful way of helping others discover you. I've written many articles, for free, for all sorts of publications, and I work hard at having books I've written available in bookstores. Why? Because business people read these articles or books, reach the conclusion that I am the expert who can help them, and then seek me out. If I sought them out and put the same information in front of them, as a sales letter or brochure or even by giving them my books, that would not have a tenth of the impact as when they discover the information for themselves.

How does that apply to you? Let's say you're a car salesperson. You can write an article or a regular column for your community newspaper about the inside secrets of buying, trading in, selling, and financing automobiles. You can write about the tax benefits of buying versus leasing and vice versa, what to look for when buying a used car, how to sell your own car, and so on. If you write a whole series of such articles, there may be newspapers, magazines, "shoppers," local union newsletters, and other publications that would be thrilled to publish them.

You could also write a book. Need ideas? How about *Confessions of a Car Salesperson: How to REALLY Get The Best Deal*, or *How To Help Your Teenager Buy and Care for That First Car*, or *Everything Women Should Know Before Buying a Car*. Then you could have that book printed and bound and donate a half-dozen copies to every branch library within 100 miles of where you sell cars. Get local bookstores to take them on consignment. Get a busy local car wash to give them away as gifts to their customers. You could even advertise and sell the book by mail.

Years ago I consulted with Dr. Robert Kotler, a cosmetic surgeon in Beverly Hills, California, who wrote and published his own book, brilliantly titled *The Consumer's Guide to Cosmetic Surgery*. Thanks to that book and its well-chosen title, he had the credibility of an author. The book got him invited on local talk shows and invited to lecture. He advertised the book rather than directly advertising his practice, and it ranks as one of the best things he ever did for his business. He's since become really famous—including a stint for a couple seasons on the popular TV show, *Dr. 90210*. I have used *The Consumer's Guide To . . .* , *The Official Guide To . . .* , or *The Insider's Guide To . . .* idea in creating hundreds of different comparable selling tools for clients in many different fields. One even landed its author, the owner of a handyman services company, on *Oprah*.

In addition to or instead of your own book, you might write for others' publications. If you sell business-to-business, for example, selling advertising time for a radio station, you could write a series of articles about the how-to's of radio advertising and then do everything possible to get them published in local business journals, newsletters, newspapers, and magazines. You could also write and publish a newsletter about the success stories of radio advertising to send out to your clients and selected prospects every month.

Today, there are many nonbook self-publishing and self-syndication options in online media, notably beginning with your own blog and strategic contributions to other blogs. The internet has made it easy for everyone to publish, to such an extent that some blogs have achieved equal status with newspapers and news magazines. While I would insist none of this packs the punch of a book, it is all worth doing.

Public Speaking

Public speaking is another very effective way to attract favorable attention from people qualified to do business with you. It is also efficient because of the numbers of people reached via each speech.

Open up your local or nearest major city Yellow Pages and look under Associations or Clubs. In one of the cities where I live, there are over 2,500 listings in this section of the phone book.

There are business groups, civic groups, and special interest groups. Most have monthly meetings. Most need speakers. Most don't pay their speakers.

If I'm that car salesperson, and I have a speech—*Confessions of a Car Salesman: How To Get a REALLY Great Deal*—I would contact local chapters of national associations and local groups, starting with the A's, the Agri-Business Council, The American Citizen and Lawmen Association, the American Legion Posts, the American Subcontractors, the Association of Realtors, and so on. You get the idea. I'd say to these groups: "Listen, I've got a 30 to 45 minute speech that's fun, funny, and will save your members money the next time they go to buy a car."

Even though I get paid to speak, as a professional, I still say no to some engagements and yes to others based on how well they position me to be discovered by good, prospective clients. For ten consecutive years I appeared in 25 to 30 cities a year with Zig Ziglar on big, public seminars, with up to 35,000 people in attendance. So why would I travel all the way from Phoenix to Key West, Florida, on a weekend, to speak to 65 people for a lot less immediate income than I get from one of these events with Zig? Because most of those 65 people had paid $7,000.00 EACH to come to a week-long, intensive seminar to learn how to apply new kinds of direct-marketing methods to their established, existent businesses. They were highly qualified prospects for a number of my professional services. By speaking there, I let them discover me.

Thirty-five years ago, when I was just getting started in public speaking, I had limited financial resources for promotion, but I had a lot of time. I did my own telemarketing and spoke for free at in-office sales meetings, real estate offices, insurance offices, and other businesses. In those speeches, I promoted my own seminars. In one year, I did over 150 of these little presentations. I improved my presentations with the practice and I made over $100,000.00 from promoting my seminars.

Just about anybody could use this same strategy. My Platinum Member Dennis Tubbergen has an entire company devoted to helping financial advisors fill seats at seminars where they can deliver the canned, proven presentations he provides, to attract key, targeted clients, like large sum IRA account holders. And it is relatively common to see "high transaction" sales professionals like investment brokers, as well as cosmetic surgeons and cosmetic dentists, putting on seminars to attract clients or patients. But I've taught hardware store owners, golf school owners, and home security system salespeople—to name a few— how to effectively sell through seminars. We have a Member very effectively promoting her restaurant, another promoting her wine business, both by speaking to women's clubs.

Big Breakthrough from Seminars

From Glazer-Kennedy Insider's Circle DIAMOND Member Peter Ursel M.D., Ontario, Canada: "I'm a cosmetic surgeon and I've been getting your *No B.S. Marketing Letter* for many years now, and have used your concepts haphazardly with pretty good results. I was happy but not ecstatic. Now I've had a breakthrough! I decided to put on a 'What's New In Cosmetic Surgery Seminar.' I did a classic Kennedy style promotion. I announced it in my monthly newsletter, I put a tabloid style, 'unprofessional' ad in the newspaper, I recycled the ad as a postcard to my list, and finally did a voice blast to my list. Results: 300 registered, 250 showed up, 140 booked appointments, and so far, over $100,000.00 in procedures! All this in a little town of 20,000 people."

Today, just as the internet has provided a portfolio of media for writing and publishing other than books, newspapers, and magazines, the internet and other technology has provided new alternative ways to use public speaking to promote businesses. Last year, my companies and my clients, combined, brought more than 10-million people to "teleseminars" and "webinars" and other "online events" for promotion and for direct sale of everything from my newest book to laparoscopic surgery to computer software systems to investments. The online events quite often feature a speaker delivering a live presentation, even writing on a whiteboard, and ending by taking questions from viewers. These speaking-via-media opportunities can erase traditional geographic boundaries of business, allow you to present to small groups efficiently and cost efficiently, and enable you to offer an interesting, alternative way for people to learn about what you do or about your products and services without putting themselves in an intimidating or uncomfortable sales environment, like an actual seminar room at a hotel or a classroom at your store, office, or showroom. They also make you a bit of a TV star, and that never hurts.

For Glazer-Kennedy Insider's Circle™ Members, we have a wide range of resources, home study courses, and assistance for people who want to master persuasive public speaking and use tele-seminars, webinars, and similar media, all accessible with free trial membership at FreeGiftFrom.com.sales.

Publicity

Publicity can change your entire life experience as a sales professional. When somebody writes an article about you and it is published in a newspaper or a magazine, or you appear as a guest on a radio or TV show, you gain credibility, authority *and* celebrity.

I believe any sales pro, selling anything, should make a concerted effort to utilize publicity, to get media exposure, to "get famous" to some degree: because we live in a celebrity and fame dominated culture. "Celebrity" is the most powerful marketing force I know of.

Most sales professionals don't need "as seen on *Oprah*" level fame in order to be accorded celebrity status by the customers important to them. **Being famous to a few will usually do**. I can still walk through airports, shopping malls and hotel lobbies without being mobbed by groupies or accosted by paparazzi, but within communities that matter to me—such as entrepreneurs passionately interested in direct marketing—my name is known, I'm referenced and talked about constantly, there are even internet sites where people gather just to talk about me, and at certain conventions and conferences I am mobbed by fans—including those asking for autographs. If you doubt my fame, just Google® me. I call myself a famous person nobody's ever heard of. I seek publicity and celebrity only selectively and strategically. You can do the same. The smaller the pond chosen, the easier and faster you can become the big fish.

Determine who your customers listen to and consider influential, what they read and consider most authoritative, what websites they visit most, and work at being interviewed by, quoted by, published in those venues.

Here's why all this—positioning, writing, speaking, selective publicity— is so important.

Are You Just Another Salesperson?

You might have the solution to a client's greatest need, the answer to his or her most earnest desire, but if you are perceived as "just another salesperson," the client won't pay attention to you or will feel hesitant about placing trust in you. That's what these techniques are all about: positioning yourself in clients' minds as the trustworthy, respected, and celebrated expert so that they seek you.

By now you may be wondering how to apply some of these ideas to your own business. These ideas are transferable, nearly universal strategies that anyone can use. Suppose, for example, you run a home security systems business.

Easy. Write a book: *Burglars' Seven Secrets for Picking the Houses and Families They Attack.* Write a column for your community newspaper: *Crimestopper Tips.* And so on.

You'll find that, just as I said earlier, the writing of a book or a newspaper column will generate business. But you can also use your book to get onto some of the talk shows. Then, watch the news for a new reason why you should appear and be interviewed again, such as a string of robberies occurring in a neighborhood and going unsolved, or the annual release to the media of the crime statistics report.

Next you could target an appropriate geographic area and start sending a quality newsletter to all the homeowners. Call it *Smart Strategies for Safe Living: How to Safeguard Your Family and Your Home.* Provide useful information and tips. Offer your book free.

You could use your book and newsletter to contact and keep contacting reporters, columnists, and editors of every publication in your area as well as talk show hosts and program directors of radio and TV stations. Be polite but persistent. You'll get written about. You'll get publicity. Then you can quote what they say about you. You might wind up with a selling asset like this: *The Cleveland Plain Dealer* said "Robert Bogart knows more about keeping burglars out than the burglars know about getting in!" That single quote from the Cleveland daily newspaper is a very valuable asset this security system salesman can use and profit from enormously, for years to come.

Another publicity idea for your business would be to exploit your success stories. Suppose shortly after you sell and install a security system in the Browns' home a burglar tries to get in, and is scared away by the alarms. When Ms. Brown calls to thank you with this story, grab your video camera, get out there, and get her testimonial on videotape. With her permission, you might issue a news release to local media, get an article published, then even mail copies to the neighbors.

Now, how do you use all this? Well, let me give you one possible scenario, what I would do in this position. When a call comes in from a homeowner asking me about a security system for his home, I would say: "Mr. Homeowner, I'm extremely busy and cannot do justice to your questions today. However, I have a complete information kit that I'll send to you, and I ask that you review it carefully. Then if you think I'm the right expert to assist you with your home security, call me back. If you choose another source, the information will still help you."

Then I would have a messenger deliver a nice, big box to Mr. Homeowner. Inside the box would be my information kit, which would include:

1. A copy of my book on home security.
2. An audio CD of highlights from my best radio talk show interview.
3. A couple of copies of my newsletter.
4. A page of quotes, "What the Media Says about Dan Kennedy, Home Security Expert."
5. A page that looks like an article about the Browns', headlined: *Even Though We Thought It Would Never Happen to Us, If We Had Waited Just Three More Days, Our Home Would Have Been Cleaned Out by Burglars!*
6. A page titled: "All Sources of Security Assistance Are NOT Equal," which lists your "credibility items" and statistics.
7. A list of famous clients and client testimonials.

Finally, and this is very important, I would include a certificate waiving my usual $250.00 fee for a home and family protection consultation.

My term for this is a "shock and awe box," so named because it's a (pleasant) shock for the consumer to get such a comprehensive collection of nicely presented information, when, at best, he might get a brochure from others, and everything in it building up your status is intended to create awe.

Now, when Mr. Homeowner calls me, what will the positioning be like? Will he perceive me as "just another salesperson?" Not likely.

The Final Component

Pain—the desire to get relief from pain, physical pain, emotional pain, or financial pain—is the strongest motivational power of all. From the top-of-the-tower corporate boardroom to the working person's small apartment, people are most moved to stop pain.

I want two things when I'm selling. First, I want someone who knows he or she has a problem that is causing some pain and, second, I want someone who perceives me as the person best qualified and most likely to solve that problem and end that pain.

In the example above of the home security business, I first want the prospective client to call me because he or she feels a need for protection. Then, I want to use "tools," not my time and energy, to let the client arrive at the conclusion that I'm the person best qualified to help take care of that need.

"Gee, This Sounds Like a Lot of Work"

Well, I guess it is a lot of work. But when you compare it to all the work inherent in old-fashioned, traditional prospecting, you'll see that my methods provide a better, continuing pay-off for effort invested. With my methods, the work is front end loaded—you have to do a lot of work to assemble your tools, engineer your system, and get it functional, up and running. But then it does a lot of work for you. If you stick to the old ways, you have to do a lot of work, the same work, work that inevitably becomes mind-numbing, energy-sapping drudgery over and over and over again, day after excruciating day.

Sales professionals dependent on traditional prospecting have to go to sleep most nights wondering where their next prospect is coming from. They get up most mornings without anybody waiting for them to sell to. These salespeople spend a lot of time hanging around the office, at the coffee shop counter and, in the afternoons, at the movie theater, avoiding prospecting. Then they spend a lot of time doing manual labor prospecting, usually when desperate. Ultimately, they spend comparatively little time selling.

The sales professional who masters my methods goes to sleep most nights booked solid for the next day with appointments, with people very likely to buy from him or her.

This is more than a choice of business strategies. This is a lifestyle choice.

CHAPTER 17

HOW TO USE "LEAD GENERATION ADVERTISING" TO ATTRACT HIGHLY QUALIFIED PROSPECTS

For more than 25 years, I have been teaching a very specific method for sales professionals of every stripe to end cold prospecting altogether, and only go where invited, only call those who've called them first. This method has been adopted, taught, and proliferated in over 250 different sales niches, by my students-turned-masters, practitioners-turned-teachers themselves. These niches include obvious sales businesses like life, health, property and casualty and business insurance, financial services, residential and commercial real estate, mortgages, home furnishings and interior decorating, automobiles, RVs, yachts, fractional jet ownership, technology products and services, as well as professional practices—health, law, accounting, and unobvious sales businesses, such as restaurants, resorts and country clubs, art galleries, charitable and nonprofit organizations, universities, and even funeral parlors. In every one of these categories there are not only thousands of business owners and sales professionals using this very specific method, there are experts who've learned it from me and now teach it.

In this chapter, I want to introduce you to this method and try to sell you on using it. It can revolutionize your experience in selling.

Never the Pest, Always the Welcome Guest

Business-to-business sales professionals are always worrying about "how to get past the gatekeeper," and I'm often asked, when hired to speak to sales groups, to answer that question. I refuse, because it's the wrong question. It suggests both artifice and difficulty, and I like neither. Instead, the superior question is:

**"How can I get sought after and invited
in by the decision maker? "**

Regardless of whether you sell B2B or to consumers, my underlying premise is to engineer a situation where you are sought out, invited in, and welcomed as an expert advisor.

Any sales trainer who is still directing you down the "101 tricks for sneaking past the gatekeeper" path should be studiously IGNORED!

The "Welcome Guest Process" in Brief

The process, presented here in very abbreviated form, is actually quite simple. It begins with Step One, one way or another, getting the qualified, interested prospect to raise his hand. Step Two is then to send him information that raises his interest level and "pre-sells" you and sells the value of the appointment itself. Step

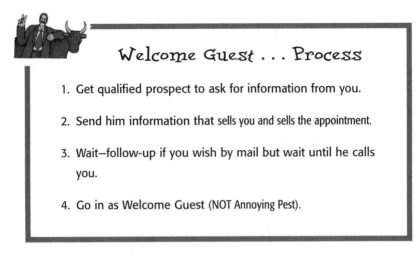

Welcome Guest ... Process

1. Get qualified prospect to ask for information from you.

2. Send him information that sells you and sells the appointment.

3. Wait—follow-up if you wish by mail but wait until he calls you.

4. Go in as Welcome Guest (NOT Annoying Pest).

Three is not to call him, but only to go and sell to him after he calls you and asks you to do so.

Successfully implemented and religiously adhered to, this changes the entire life of the sales pro. It multiplies income, because your time is not wasted, your energy not wasted, stress is replaced with pleasure, closing rates skyrocket, transaction size increases, referrals are easier to obtain. In The New Economy, life for the unwelcome, uninvited pest is going to be even more miserable than in prior years. There will always be salespeople grinding out a living in this role, pests so persistent, with stamina so super-human, they cannot be stopped. But do you really want to make your living thanks to high tolerance for pain?

The Welcome Guest Approach is ideally suited to the "mind-set" of The New Economy Customer. He is more resistant than ever to the salesman literally or figuratively knocking on his door, striving to be more circumspect in choosing what he buys and who he buys from, and conditioned by recession to spending reluctance. The arrival of "another salesman" is therefore perceived *as a threat*. The salesperson who pushes his way past guards and resistance to pitch a product is going to start out with enormous disadvantage to overcome. Conversely, this same New Economy Customer is less confident about his decision-making, purchasing, and investing thanks to his recession experiences, and more receptive than ever to valid, valuable advice from someone he feels he can trust and who he views as a bona-fide expert, a highly competent professional. The salesperson invited in, in that role, begins with enormous advantage.

To begin, then, Step One is called "lead generation." Through an ad, a letter, a postcard, or other means, a qualified lead is produced. That means, a person qualified to buy has stepped forward and asked to be provided with information.

How a Lead Generation Ad Works Like a "Personals" Ad

If you've ever read, written, or responded to a "personals" ad, you know that they are written to do two things: attract responses from carefully described people and discourage responses from those who do not meet the desired qualifications. The ad might run something like this:

SINGLE WHITE FEMALE seeks single or divorced man,
35 to 49, confident, established in his career,
who enjoys travel, theater, cooking, cuddling.
No smokers or heavy drinkers, please.

This same approach works for most products or services. You can target your prospect with a lead generation ad. For example, a financial planner might place the following ad:

WARNING FOR MARRIED OWNERS OF BUSINESSES,
EXECUTIVES, AND ENTREPRENEURS WITH
TAXABLE INCOMES OVER $250,000.00 PER YEAR:
YOU are the government's #1 target. Your net,
combined tax load could as much as DOUBLE in the
next 12 months. Your pension fund or retirement
savings is at new risk. Do you know the TRUTH about
the government's plans for your hard-earned money?
MY FREE REPORT: "FINANCIAL ALERT!" reveals the
details in plain English (NOT financial gobbledygook)
and provides important strategies and tips. If you
earn over $250,000.00, own a business, own your
own home, and have a pension or retirement savings
plan, this report is for you. CALL: a free recording
message at 000-000-0000 or request your Report
online at www.TaxAlert.com

Clearly this ad "telegraphs" to certain people, and excludes many others, just like a personals ad. Notice the ad does NOT talk about the planner or about products, services, or a particular company.

The person who responds to this ad tells the planner several very important things. He or she is married, owns or runs a business, earns over $250,000.00 a year, owns (or is buying) a home, is saving for retirement, is concerned about taxes, is no fan of the current government administration, and is anxious about his finances. The person responding to this ad meets demographic qualifications and a mind-set profile. And most importantly, the person responding feels he is taking the first step.

Given all this knowledge about this prospect, the financial planner can create a free report* that directly "hits" this person right where he feels it most. The planner then sends the report with the package of promotional materials* (see Chapter 17, where such a package is described in the example of the security system salesperson). This establishes the planner in the right role I've described in this chapter, with the right positioning, described in the previous chapter. Importantly, it avoids the normal salesperson behavior: jumping on the phone with the prospect the instant he shows himself, pushing for an appointment immediately.

When the phone rings—and it will—you can be sure that this financial planner is already well-positioned. The prospective client won't be looking at "just another salesperson"—he will be seeking out this planner as the expert most likely to solve personal financial concerns.

Where Do You Run Lead Generation Advertising?

If you sell products or services to businesses, you may use local area business journals and legal newspapers, the business section of your city's daily newspaper, or the trade magazines that serve your clients' type of business. As you probably know, there are national or international trade magazines for virtually every type of business and industry, from aluminum manufacturing to zebra breeding. Also, just about every business has at least one association that publishes and usually offers advertising in a newsletter that goes to its members.

If you sell products to the general public, you might use your city's daily newspaper, weekly community newspapers, local "shoppers," broadcast media (radio or TV), or coupon packs delivered to residences, like Money Mailer or ValPak.

---

*This free report is the equivalent of a sales letter. The techniques for writing such letters are fully described in another book of mine, *The Ultimate Sales Letter* (published by Adams Media and available in bookstores).

You can also do this kind of lead generation advertising online, in many venues. Here is a secret to keep in mind: the highest productivity comes from treating the website or sites, purchased traffic, everything done online only as another lead generation media, then doing follow-up offline, via paper 'n ink direct mail (not by e-mail).

The real answer to where to do your lead generation advertising is: where your ideal prospect frequents, in what he reads, watches, or listens to.

The Postcard Technique

Many salespeople get great results putting their lead generation ad onto a simple postcard and mailing it to lists of likely prospects. The postcard is just about the simplest, least costly advertising vehicle you can find when you consider the cost of a postage stamp.

If you sell to consumers, there are all sorts of mailing lists readily available to you from the very simple, such as all the homeowners in a particular postal region, to something quite complicated, like a "merge-purged" list of subscribers to home decorating magazines who have credit cards, own the homes they live in, and fall into certain age and income ranges, in particular postal regions.

Lists are also available for business buyers including subscribers to certain trade magazines or other publications, compiled lists of business owners or executives by size of business, type of business, annual sales, number of employees, and other criteria.

In most cities, you'll find List Brokers as a heading in the Yellow Pages; one of these local brokers can probably handle simple, local list needs. If you're interested in something more sophisticated, it will pay you to learn a bit about all the lists and list-related services that are available, at SRDS.com. Spending an hour or so going through SRDS will open your eyes to a whole world of opportunity! Basically, if you can describe ideal prospects, you can find available lists to match. And, generally, money spent in list selection is money well spent.

Headlines Are Important

Here's a simple "copy secret" for making these ads, letters, websites, and postcards work: The headline is the single most important part of the postcard. For example:

CONGRATULATIONS!
YOU'VE ALREADY WON:

Then you continue:

You've been selected to
receive a fascinating FREE REPORT about
(insert your title).

Then you drop in the rest of your lead generation ad's message. Here's a complete example:

CONGRATULATIONS!
YOU'VE ALREADY WON:

You've been selected to receive a copy of automotive expert Bill Gizmo's informative book, *How to Keep Your Car Alive & Kicking at Minimum Cost, Without Ever Getting Burnt by Repair Rip-Offs,* absolutely FREE.

This book is a $9.95 publisher's price value, and it is full of insider information that can save every member of your family money. After all, your family's car(s) represents one of the five biggest investments of your entire life.

Shouldn't you know what insiders—mechanics, race car drivers—know about keeping cars 100% healthy at minimum cost?

Your FREE COPY of this book will be sent to you by mail. There is no cost, no obligation, no strings attached. (This is part of a consumer interest test.) To get your free book, just call (000) 000-0000 and leave your name and address on the recording as instructed or visit www.FreeCarBook.com

---

Who Uses Lead Generation Advertising?

Look around. Big, brand name companies that sell by appointment or by bringing customers into showrooms use it a lot. Tempur-Pedic and "Sleep Number" beds, for example. I dare you to pick any magazine off the newsstand and not find these kinds of ads. But not nearly as noticeable, the continent is full of observant, savvy salespeople who have taken note of this model and applied it to their own businesses and careers.

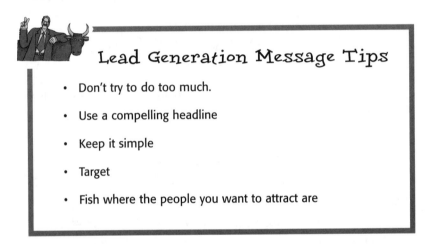

Lead Generation Message Tips

- Don't try to do too much.

- Use a compelling headline

- Keep it simple

- Target

- Fish where the people you want to attract are

Here are the secrets to making lead generation advertising work for you, too:

- *Don't try to accomplish too much.* The only job of lead generation is to produce leads. Do not try to "pre-sell" your product or service, build business name recognition, or otherwise achieve multiple objectives. Focus 100% on getting the right people to respond. Simply getting the right people to step forward, raise their hands, and identify themselves to you is enough.
- *Use a powerful, attention-grabbing headline.* Remember that the headline must be clear, bold, and simple. It usually

should telegraph the promise of a great benefit. And it's very hard to beat "free" as a component part of what you are offering.

- *Keep it simple.* There's no need to complicate this at all. Focus on a straightforward offer such as a free report, booklet, book, or CD, all of which work very well. Sometimes a free consultation of some kind will work.
- *TARGET!* Write your message to exclude many and attract the relatively few who are perfectly matched with what you have to offer.
- *FISH* where the people you want to attract swim.

How to Use Lead Generation to Force Prospects to Give You Information and Grant Your Control of the Sales Process

One of my longtime Members is a marketing and sales consultant for technology and industrial companies, marketing business-to-business, and he specializes in online lead generation. He sent me results from a "split-test" conducted for a manufacturer selling to engineers. If you aren't familiar with the idea of split-testing, it means changing only one variable in an ad, letter, website, phone script, etc. and trying version #1 on half the leads, version #2 on the other. On the internet it's easy to do, as alternating site visitors can be automatically split up and sent to different versions of the same landing page or complete site without them knowing it.

Anyway, one version of this company's site provided a typical brochure online, featuring a Q&A presentation of the company's capabilities and technology applications. The radically different version offered only a "tease" page with a barrier to entry to more information. This page offered basically the same information repositioned as special reports for the engineers, but required the site visitor to provide complete contact information and answers to a few key questions before they could get to the special reports.

You might think this would suppress response and in many instances you'd be right, although that might not be a bad thing. Disqualifying only casually interested prospects is often very desirable. But in this case, the opposite occurred. The traditional site was converting only 3.5% of the visitors to prospects requesting more information and/or appointments. The new site converted 36.9% of the visitors to real leads. And the ultimate conversions to sales were also higher with the second group than the first.

The Last but First Thing You Need to Know About Lead Generation

Lead generation is about "bait."

It requires a match of the right bait to attract the right critter. If you want a backyard full of deer, do not put a big 500-pound block of cheddar cheese out there. Your backyard will soon be overrun with rats and mice. If you want deer, try a salt block. However if you want rodents, nix the salt, use the cheese. You can attract any critter to your backyard with the right bait. Similarly you can get anyone you desire to respond to lead generation advertising, direct-mail, and other media—Fortune 500 CEOs, surgeons, stay-at-home moms—if you get the bait right. If you fail, you're using the wrong bait.

Special Note: The following story from guest contributors Jimmy Vee and Travis Miller illustrates the principles of Chapters 16 and 17 in action. These principles are so powerful these business partners were able to go from struggling to successful sales professionals to owners of thriving companies to expert advisors and trainers in this field, even authors of their own book, *Gravitational Marketing*. I'm pleased to say that they have been "Kennedy students" and Members for many years.

How to Go From Zero Dollars and Zero Customers to a Million Dollar Business, Fast—In The New Economy

By Jimmy Vee and Travis Miller

Several years ago we had no customers, no prospects, and no leads. Travis' wedding was six weeks away. Jim's was six months away and there was no way either of our fiancées wanted to marry a broke loser.

We had just left the comfort and security of our high-paying jobs to strike out on our own and try to make it as entrepreneurs. We started our first company with $200.00. We bought a phone and the bank charged us a fee to have the account. We were fast on our way to losing money.

We knew we had to do something and do it fast with less than $200.00.

You may be in a similar position now or remember when you were. It's do-or-die, gun-to-the-head, make-it-or-break-it business success in its purest form. You need to attract customers immediately or fail. There is no in between.

The Most Frightening Time in Your Life

It can be the most frightening time in a business owner's life. You have to come home in the evening and face your family, then wake up in the morning and face yourself in the mirror . . . knowing that today will be the same as yesterday. No new opportunities, no new prospects, and no money at the end of the week. Sometimes it feels like the entire weight of the world is on your shoulders.

There Is a Better Approach to Selling

You need to forget the things they taught you in college, in business school, in sales training, or in orientation at your new job.

Instead you can create an intelligent system that positions you as an expert and causes qualified and interested prospects to come to you and ask you to do business with them . . . even in recession or in the emerging New Economy. A system that stops you from having to do all the ordinary sales grunt work like dropping all of those cheesy lines, popping in on people, bothering people, and calling them 25 times just so you can get a return call.

We've Been Exactly Where You Are Right Now

We know how you feel. We've been there before. Like during our first two months in business, when we relied heavily on the telephone as a marketing tool. When we got a warm lead, we would pounce and make sure the lead didn't get away. One time we made a total of 27 calls to the same individual. We always had to leave a voicemail or got the dreaded "I'm busy now, call me tomorrow" blow off. In the end, we realized the guy was just stringing us along so he didn't hurt our feelings.

Now, years later, this same guy pops up again. This time, he was pulled in and automatically converted to a sale on one of our most expensive products and we never spoke to him on the phone a single time. Everything happened automatically.

This fellow doesn't even know that we (people he now perceives as top experts in the field) are the same two pests who harassed him every day for a month practically begging for his business. Clearly, our new method is far superior to the original, conventional method.

Attract Clients Naturally

So what is this new method that allows you to easily and effortlessly attract new leads, positions you as an expert instead of a product pusher, allows you to accelerate your business growth and your success and finally begin to enjoy life and prosper a bit?

Let us explain. Thankfully, when we began, we already knew a thing or two about effective marketing. In our careers as marketing executives, we had worked together to create campaigns and systems for our clients that made many business owners instant successes. In total, we had invested $96-million of our clients' money and with that generated more than $12-billion in sales. It wasn't our money to spend or keep so we didn't get rich. But we did learn an awful lot in the process about how to attract customers and make them buy.

Armed with that knowledge, experience, and just less than $200.00, we went to work creating our dream and our fortune. We asked, "How can we duplicate the results we created for our clients and cause people to come to us but without spending a lot of money?"

So we locked ourselves in our office, which happened to be a 10x10 room in one of our houses. Everyday for months and months we would hole away in that office with the door shut and try to solve this problem.

We tried different ideas and we tested different techniques and we presented different theories. And then one day it all came to us at once.

The Eureka Moment

This simple, little idea would truly make people quickly, easily, and naturally come to you and identify themselves, almost waving their hands, saying "I want what you have to sell." Then you could put all of your focus, energy, budget and time marketing directly to those people who have already told you that they want what you have to offer, that they want the benefit that you offer, and they've given you permission to tell them about it.

That sale has almost no friction, a higher closing ratio, and typically is more enjoyable to make. It also provides you a customer with a longer relationship span who has a higher degree of respect for you and your company, which is very important, and a greater level of profitability to your company, which is extremely important.

This process, which we called Gravitational Marketing, causes potential customers to raise their hands and say, "Market to me because this is something I'm interested in." That is a powerful thing.

Don't Envy Us . . . Join Us

Fast forward to the present and you'll see that we have made it. We've turned that first $200.00 into multiple successful companies and millions of dollars in annual revenue which gives us the freedom and flexibility to spend time with our families, live life on our own terms, and leave a legacy while living a legacy by helping other business owners, entrepreneurs, and sales and marketing professionals achieve the success they're after.

The Power of Gravitational Marketing

Gravitational Marketing is based on the principle that all bodies exhibit an inherent force called gravity that naturally attracts other bodies. Following that analogy, every business has a natural tendency, however large or small, to attract customers. Larger companies traditionally have a stronger gravitational force. Smaller companies traditionally have a weaker gravitational force. This force is created by several factors such as a company's general existence, location, signage, current and past marketing and advertising efforts and word-of-mouth. As the force grows, it builds momentum and allows you to attract exactly the right group of prospects and customers without wasting tons of money.

Our method levels the playing field and gives businesses and sales professionals that have limited marketing and sales resources an opportunity to increase their gravitational potential. Continuing the analogy, Gravitational Marketing helps companies defy the laws of gravity by attracting more than their fair share of the business.

Gravitational Marketing is the process of motivating prospects to ask for your marketing messages, forging emotional relationships with them, getting your newly formed friends to buy, motivating existing customers to return, and ultimately motivating all of your customers to tell others, thereby harnessing the power of word-of-mouth advertising, which we all know is the best and cheapest form of marketing.

How Gravitational Marketing Works

The process of Gravitational Marketing is broken down into four primary components: Gravitate, Captivate, Invigorate, and Motivate.

Gravitate

The process begins first by either choosing who it is that your existing product or service would be right for or finding the who first and then determining what they want.

Next you find out what problems they're having, what difficulties and challenges they face, or what they really want but have to live without. And you offer the solution to that problem, whatever it is.

For instance, if you are a financial planner, then the people that you're going to help want security, they want to retire wealthy, and they want to retire early. They don't know how to accomplish these things. That's their problem.

If you're a real estate agent, the clients you will help want to sell their homes as quickly as possible for as much as possible or own as much home as possible for the lowest payment possible. That's what they want from you. Nothing else.

If you're a car dealer, the people you want to help are afraid of getting taken advantage of when buying a car. They want to make sure that they get the best deal possible.

The list goes on and on. So you offer a very simple initial solution that only requires a small step, a small type of action with little commitment and zero risk.

It's almost like a piece of bait. It's like saying, "I've got the answer to your problem—come to me and I'll explain."

At first glance, this may seem like regular advertising, but indeed, it is very different.

Captivate
The Captivate phase happens once you've gotten your prospects' attention. They've asked for more information about the solution that you're offering and you have a chance to present yourself to them. But you have to present yourself in a way that is unforgettable. You

can't just be another "me too" service or a commodity product. You've got to be sensational. You've got to be memorable. You've got to be unique. You must captivate your audience in order to hold their attention, arouse child-like curiosity in them, and cause them to be intrigued and to want to know more.

Invigorate

You Invigorate your prospects by helping them understand how bad the problem actually is that they're facing now and how wonderful the solution really could be. You must get them to visualize themselves living the dream.

You need to involve their emotions in the process and help them understand the depth of their problem but also the true availability of the solution and the wonderful things that will come with the solution.

Motivate

Finally, you have to Motivate your prospects to take the action you want them to take. That means you have to know ahead of time what that action should be. You can't just willy-nilly get to the Motivate phase and not know how to proceed and let the prospect direct the transaction.

Each step of this process is critical. If you fail to attract prospects (Gravitate) in the first place nothing will happen. But once you've attracted the prospect, if you don't capture their attention (Captivate) you will become invisible and the sale will be lost. Even if you have captured their attention, if you don't involve their emotions and get them excited (Invigorate) about the possibility and potential of working together, the game is over. Finally, if everything has come together but you don't cause the prospect to take the final action (Motivate), if you don't ask them to spend money, all of your efforts will have been wasted.

What To Do Today to Make Money Tomorrow

All this sounds great, but we know that action is what creates business success. As Elvis said, "A little less conversation, a little more action." So we're going to give you a down and dirty, step-by-step action plan for creating your own Gravitational Marketing campaign.

Step 1: Be Sensational

The first step is to learn to be unforgettable. Be the kind of sales professional people want to get more of. Same is lame. Boring is invisible. Sensational people and businesses attract more than their fair share of the business. They Gravitate prospects and customers naturally with less effort and expense.

How can you be sensational? Simple.

- Be interested in other people.

- Be unique enough to remember.

- Be fun to be around and do business with.

- Be willing to take risks and try new things.

- Be visible to the right people as frequently as you can.

- Be credible, by doing what you say you're going to do and get testimonials from past clients that prove your credibility.

- Be spreadable—that is, be worth talking about and worth recommending.

Step 2: Position Yourself as an Expert

Let's face it, people don't like to be sold. But they love to buy things. And who do people most want to do business with? Experts. It's the difference between being a specialist and a generalist. People will

---

New Economy Success Secret:
Careful Spending Doesn't Necessarily Mean Less Spending

The worry we talked about earlier manifests itself as more careful spending, not necessarily less spending. People who are spending more carefully are looking for two things before they spend: confidence and value. Your job as a business owner and marketer is to increase confidence and deliver more value.

How do you do this? You can increase confidence by positioning yourself as an expert, creating a clearly defined buying preference for your product or service so the decision to choose you is easy, creating expert information to help smooth the buying process, building better relationships with your customers before and after the sale, and differentiating yourself from competition.

With an increase in confidence comes an increase in value. Value can further be increased by educating your customer in addition to selling your customer, by improving and enhancing your experience, and by engaging in better follow-up.

Finding new ways to increase confidence and value is a key to success in The New Economy.

---

pay more for a specialist, they'll feel more comfortable during a transaction with a specialist, and they are more receptive to doing business in the first place with a specialist. In the end, people are more satisfied after working with an expert and more likely to tell others.

How can you become an expert? Declare yourself an expert today, do some research tonight, and start acting like one tomorrow. Understand that you know more about your business than most other people in the world. That alone makes you an expert. There's no sense waiting for someone else to come and pin an expert button on your chest or bake you a special cookie. So you may as well do it yourself.

Step 3: Determine Who You Want to Attract

You can't do business with everyone, so determine who wants what you have to sell most and target them specifically. Your gravitational power is much greater if you narrow your efforts to a specific group of people.

You'll be able to hone your message to match your prospects' wants, needs, and desires. You'll be able to increase your visibility and credibility with a small group much more quickly than you can a large group.

Step 4: Know What Sets You Apart

Determine what unique emotional appeals and benefits your product or service delivers to your target. Create your marketing message around this uniqueness and stick to it. Don't get caught up with features or image or pricing. Instead, lock on to your prospects' emotional desires and craft a message around it.

Gravitational Marketing in The New Economy

All that sounds great, but what about The New Economy? Everything is different and we'll probably never go back. Radically and swiftly changing economic conditions, evolving customers, and a dramatic power shift from rich companies and powerful media to ordinary consumers. These changes are viewed by many as a cause for panic and fear. But with the right strategies The New Economy can be a tremendous opportunity for wealth and prosperity. Gravitational Marketing is now more important than ever.

Jimmy Vee and Travis Miller are the nation's leading experts on attracting customers and the authors of *Gravitational Marketing: The Science of Attracting Customers* (Wiley). Get their FREE customer attraction starter pack at www.GravitationalMarketing.com.

Gravitational Marketing is a registered trademark of Scend LLC.

PART III

A NO B.S. START-TO-FINISH
STRUCTURE FOR THE SALE

CHAPTER 18

THE SIX STEPS OF THE
NO B.S. SALES PROCESS

Before I had turned 45, I received by mail my invitation to join the American Association of Retired Persons (AARP). It was a beautiful direct-mail package, including a personalized letter, a temporary membership card embossed with my name, and a great premium offer. Only one problem: you have to be 55 to join. It arrived at my place more than a few years too soon. And no matter how great the offer is, I'm not buying.

Many salespeople waste tons of time trying to sell to people who cannot or will not buy. It's not always as clear-cut as in my case with AARP, but it still happens often, for a lot of reasons. Some salespeople are too lazy, too ignorant, or too "chicken" to properly qualify prospects. I know salespeople in business-to-business situations, for example, who know they need to be

dealing with the CEO, but insist on selling to the personnel directors, training directors, and sales managers instead. Why? It's
easier to get to those people. It takes less confidence and self-
esteem to deal with those people. The problem is that dealing
with those people is ineffective.

How do you know who is the right prospect?

- Someone who has a reason for interest in your proposi-
  tion.
- Someone with the financial ability to say yes.
- Someone with the authority to say yes.
- Someone who is predisposed to say yes.

Interest

Let me quickly explain those four qualifications: first, the
prospect has to have a logical reason for interest. Someone who
lives in the middle of the Mojave Desert is probably a poor
prospect for a yacht. A 92-year-old is probably a poor prospect
for life insurance, definitely a poor prospect for skiing lessons.
Those are obvious. The real-life situations you deal with aren't so
obvious.

I don't want to encourage you to prejudge prospects to the
extreme. However, you need to determine some sensible link
between the prospect and the proposition. If you sell furniture,
for example, "homeowner" might be the only link needed. If you
sell very high-end, expensive furniture, it might be homeowners
only in certain zip codes, with a certain size home, with a certain
amount of equity in their homes.

Ability

Second, you need someone with the financial ability to say yes. If
you sell to businesses, you might want to zero in on companies
that have reported growth in the previous quarter (which is a

reflection of their financial strength). If you sell swimming pools, aluminum siding, insurance, remodeling, etc., to homeowners, and are going to do a pre-approach letter campaign, you might want to have the mailing list of residents in a given area merged with a list of bank credit card holders. The odds are much better that credit card holders are financially able to buy.

Authority

Third, you need to talk to someone with the authority to buy. In consumer selling, that often means that both husband and wife have to be present at the meeting. In business-to-business marketing, you have to determine who has the authority to spend how much for what. It is easy to ignore this caveat and be a very busy salesperson who is not very busy selling. In my own selling, I'm usually dealing directly with an entrepreneur who has sought me out—with THE decision maker.

Predisposition

Fourth, I urge salespeople to concentrate on selling to people predisposed to say yes. In mail order, for example, we're much better off marketing to known mail-order buyers who also fit our other selection criteria than to people who perfectly fit our selection criteria but have no history of mail-order shopping. If I were selling investment or insurance services, I'd rather contact people who already had some insurance or investments than those who did not. Beyond that, using the "positioning, not prospecting" strategies presented earlier in this book, you can be sure you are investing your time only with those predisposed to buying— *from you.*

Here is the most important thing: you should create your own Highest Probability Prospect Profile, then do everything you can to invest your money and time in reaching only those people. When you combine setting out to attract or pursuing only Highest Probability Prospects with my No B.S. Sales Process, you can engineer truly spectacular results. So, the Process . . .

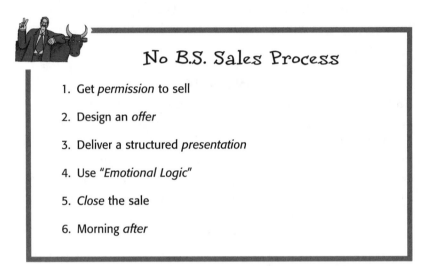

No B.S. Sales Process

1. Get *permission* to sell

2. Design an *offer*

3. Deliver a structured *presentation*

4. Use *"Emotional Logic"*

5. *Close* the sale

6. Morning *after*

Step One: Permission to Sell

The first step in the selling process can be best defined as obtaining the prospect's permission to sell. You cannot sell effectively to someone who is mentally or physically backing away from you. Nor can you successfully force someone to pay attention. A person has to choose to be sold to before you can sell to them.

The best advice for securing permission to sell is a question structured like this:

If I could show you how to

_____ would you be

interested in knowing

more about it?

Or, if you prefer to be bolder in your assumption, try this:

If I could show you how to
_____ you'd be interested
in knowing more about it, wouldn't you?

The prospect who responds positively to this question gives you permission to sell, and you will have actually built a little box around the person, with his or her cooperation, that virtually guarantees subsequently closing the sale. Now all you have to do is fulfill the "if I could show you how to" conditions, point out that you have done so, say "Eureka!" and ask your prospect to "initial right here."

Here is an actual example I scripted for a client of mine in the investment real estate business. When his reps use it, it will work like magic! It is a series of question:

- Did you pay federal income tax last year?
- Would you be interested in legally reducing the amount of taxes you pay, providing it didn't cost you anything to do so?
- Could you use $5,000.00 to $15,000.00 in extra cash income per year?
- Do you consider yourself an open-minded, positive-thinking person?
- Then, if I could show you how to legally reduce your taxes at no cost to you, increase your income, and associate with others doing the same thing, would you be interested in knowing more?

This series of questions will get the needed permission to sell more than 50% of the time. It can be used in person-to-person prospecting, telemarketing and, preferably, in lead generation advertising or direct-mail.

I have a "bonus," advanced strategy for you, one that secures permission to sell and ensures heightened interest from the prospect. A financial advisor in Chicago who uses it exactly as I scripted, targets only multimillionaire business owners, and gets invited in to meet with 92% of all he approaches. It is that powerful. I call it: guarantee the appointment. Or, buy the appointment. Here's what it reads or sounds like:

> Give me ___ minutes. If I fail to show you at least X#
> _____ you did not know about and would
> otherwise not have known about—and that your
> _____ had not told you about—and you honestly feel
> I wasted your time, just say the word, and I will pay you
> $_____ as my penalty, right on the spot, cash, on your
> desk.

Actual example of this template filled in:

> Give me 19 minutes. If I fail to show you three strategies
> for improving response to your existent advertising or
> extracting more value from your leads—that your ad
> agency has not told you about—and you honestly feel
> I wasted your time, I will pay you $500.00 . . .

That's the one I used, in 1974 and 1975, when I first started an advertising consulting business.

Today, I use a very different approach, and to be fair, I should let you see the flip side. These days, I never meet with anyone free, and any new client relationship begins a certain prescribed way. The verbiage is as follows:

> All new client relationships begin with a day of diag-
> nostic and prescriptive consulting, at my base rate,
> $18,800.00. At the end of the day, one of three things
> happens: one, we've had a good, productive day
> and you leave happy with strategies to act on. Two,

there's a project or projects you want to hire me to do for you, in which case the initial day's fee is fully credited to the larger project fees and royalties. Or three, you feel your day was unproductive, in which case I gladly refund your fee.

As you can see, I am still guaranteeing the appointment.

This is tried and true, but one of the things is even more relevant to The New Economy. In The New Economy, *everything* must be earned. There are no gimmies. Even the permission to sell must be legitimately earned. It will not be casually given to you by any prospect worth investing time in; the more valuable the prospect, the harder it will be to get. So, a very specific promise for information gained just during the initial appointment, conversation, or meeting, and a guarantee, are means of earning that permission.

Step Two: The Offer

I believe in prefabricating an easy-to-explain, clear, simple, and understandable offer that includes no more than three and preferably only two options.

A two-option offer, commonly called "an either/or" or "an A/B split" usually divides along price lines. You might have a basic, no-frills package at $X, or an options-added, deluxe package at a higher $Y. Another similar approach is to present the deluxe offer, but have a lower cost offer in reserve for a step-down sale. However you choose to structure it, you should get to a point in the sale where you lay out the "you get this and this and this and this" summary of products, services, warranties, benefits.

I am almost always opposed to cafeteria selling; letting the customer pick items from an ala carte menu. In countless situations, I've improved the average transaction size, closing percentage, and speed of sale by putting the individual items into "bundles" or "packages" and offering only the choice of Package A, B, or C.

Step Three: The Presentation

There are several "classic" formulas for the structure of a sales presentation. You can find and learn them in a variety of books, tapes, and articles. They have been tested and proven over time. You do not need any new or more sophisticated formulas. You only need to select the one most appropriate to your particular situation. But you should build your presentation with one of them.

One formula you'll hear about is **AIDA**: **A**ttention, **I**nterest, **D**esire, and **A**ction. First, you get the prospect's attention. This is most commonly done by briefly outlining a set of benefits. Next, you build interest by providing evidence of the benefits with facts, statistics, demonstrations, stories, and testimonials. Then, you create desire by relating the benefits to the prospect. You can also build desire with discounts, incentives, or premiums available for prompt action. Finally, you create action with a closing technique.

Another formula is **PAS**: **P**roblem, **A**gitate, and **S**olve. This is the formula I prefer to employ whenever possible. I was using it long before I knew what it was called or that it was, in fact, a known formula.

With this formula, you first state a problem and secure the prospect's agreement that the problem exists. For example, you might agree that there is an epidemic of crabgrass in the neighborhood. Next, you get the prospect agitated about the problem, perhaps realizing that crabgrass ruins the appearance of the lawn by damaging the root structure of the healthy grass and that it can damage the lawn mower. Then you produce the solution. Example: Wouldn't it be wonderful if there was a liquid you could spray on your lawn that actually killed crabgrass without damaging the other grass?

I want to emphasize that you should have a disciplined approach to your presentations. If you are "winging it," you're kidding yourself about being a professional. Fortunately for you, the airline pilot who flies you from place to place and the surgeon who operates on you, should you, God forbid, ever need it, don't "wing it." They are professionals.

To a More Sophisticated Approach to "Presentation"

Renowned sales communication expert Ari Galper has contributed a special discussion of presentation strategies, appearing at the end of this chapter. You can also learn more at www.UnlockTheGame.com.

Step Four: Emotional Logic

As far as I know, my speaking colleague of ten years, Zig Ziglar coined the term "emotional logic in selling." It represents the way people *really* buy: they take buying action spurred on by emotional factors, but need logical reasons to justify doing what they really feel like doing.

If you try to get somebody to reason their way to a sale with you, you're going to find tough sledding wherever you go. And I don't care if you're selling sophisticated computer systems to Fortune 500 executives, the act of buying will still occur at an emotional level. If you can't create emotional activity and feelings inside your prospect, you won't make many sales.

But you don't want to be an "emotions steamroller" either. If you do, you'll probably wind up buying back as much as you sell or selling to each customer only once and never building valuable relationships. People require reasons to justify their actions. You need to combine emotion with logic.

Use the E-Factors

There are five main Emotional Factors that motivate people to action: love, pride, fear, guilt, and greed. Please note, though, that they are all based on a simpler self-interest formula of avoiding pain and obtaining pleasure. For example, let's say you are soliciting money for a nonprofit organization. Some people might feel guilty about how well off they are compared to the world's poor starving children; they might fear bad luck or karma for not doing their share; they might take pride in being able to help; they might be genuinely inspired by love of humankind; or they might see positive public relations benefits for their business by participating. So all five factors might influence them to participate. But if you go beneath that activity to the very core of response, not giving must be more personally and emotionally painful than giving, and there must be personal and emotional pleasure from giving.

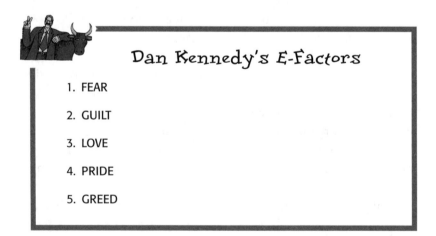

Dan Kennedy's E-Factors

1. FEAR

2. GUILT

3. LOVE

4. PRIDE

5. GREED

The savvy sales pro tries to push all of these buttons in the presentation.

Step Five: Closing the Sale

I once flew across the country seated next to a grizzled direct-sales veteran who had been a door-to-door vacuum cleaner salesman during the Depression. When hired, he had to study a huge book of answers to 357 different objections and stalls, and learn 357 different ways to close a sale, and take a test on it before getting out into the field where he could make some money. So he learned all 357. And he told me that in his entire sales career since he'd only used three of them.

I believe that closing the sale should be a natural progression, not some abrupt jack-in-the-box trick you pull out at the end. If closing is difficult, something is wrong with earlier parts of the selling process. You should not have anxiety or stress about the close because it should happen virtually of its own accord, from the momentum you've established. In my own experience, clients will ask: "OK, how do we get started?" before I even have to "close."

Also, if you've asked a series of trial close questions as you've gone along, you will have established the momentum toward the positive closing and you will have already taken the tension out of asking questions and obtaining answers.

On the other hand, I'm not suggesting you be weak-kneed about closing either. If you aren't fortunate (or good) enough that the prospect jumps ahead of you and literally says "Let's do it," then you need to accelerate your use of assumptions as you approach the close. Salespeople sell their way right out of sales by using "if" instead of "when" terminology. For example, never say "if you become a member," say "when you become a member," or better "as a member, you get . . . ." If you are meeting the prospect in person, match your words with physical action: "here in your Member Kit, you'll see . . . ."

If you must ask a closing question, there is one simple formula superior to all others. Just about the only closing question structure I bother using or teaching is the simple yes-or-yes question. Would you prefer red or blue? With or without? Today or tomorrow? Pay in three or four installments?

Some people say this is "old hat," and I guess it is. But I haven't found anything better. People usually choose from what's put in front of them. You go into a restaurant, they give you a menu, you choose from the menu. You call up the airline, they tell you what times the flights are, you choose one. So assuming everything else in the sales process has gone well, a two-option, yes-or-yes question is a comfortable way to close the process. Why fool around with anything else?

Step Six: The Morning After

Here is a secret few salespeople use—not because it is unknown to them, but because they are too lazy to use it. The secret is to ensure the satisfaction of the customer after the sale. There are several good reasons to build this step into your sales process.

First, some people suffer from "buyer's remorse." They wake up and feel differently about the purchase a day or two after the sale. The emotion of the moment is gone. They are groping for reasons to justify the action. Buyers like this need "post-sale reassurance." This can often take the form of a well-written letter that thanks a customer for his or her purchase, congratulates him or her on the purchase choice, and restates the reasons why the decision was such a good one. In direct marketing, we call this a "stick letter"—designed to make the sale stick. There's a classic example in my book, *The Ultimate Sales Letter*.

You might also send or deliver a thank-you or welcome gift, a bonus that was never discussed during the sale. Oh, and here's a secret from selling situations where there is typically a high level of buyer's remorse and/or refunds: immediately deliver a "welcome to our customer family" gift of food. Cookies, brownies, a big fruit basket, or steaks. This is the close equivalent of "breaking bread" with someone and their office staff or family. It is much harder for someone to cancel a purchase and go back on their commitment after they've eaten your food.

Second, a customer's first purchase should be the beginning of a long, happy, active relationship. You need to do little things after the sale to cement that relationship.

Finally, if you can create a system that motivates your customers or clients to refer others to you, you will never have problems building a giant income and a secure career in selling. As a matter of fact, any sales professional having to worry about prospecting after he has more than a dozen customers is, frankly, doing something wrong in the selling or post-sale satisfying of the customer. Early in my career, I heard a recording from Paul J. Meyer, the founder of Success Motivation Institute, about "the endless chain of referrals." Its premise simple: if you get one customer and he gives you at least one referral and the same is true of each subsequent customer and you never break the chain, you never run out of new customers. The reasons most sales professionals fail to own such endless chains are many, but it is because the sales professionals fail at it, not because the endless chains aren't there to be had.

This is more important than ever in The New Economy. Remember that New Economy Customers have been conditioned to be more cautious and conservative, more skeptical, and thus more difficult to obtain by all means other than a referral or recommendation from a family member, friend, associate, or peer. As the monetary costs of acquiring new customers through advertising and marketing rise, and the time costs of acquiring new customers through traditional prospecting rise, securing every possible referral grows exponentially in importance. One of the best pieces of advice for sales professionals in The New Economy is to invest a lot more of your attention in what happens after making a sale than you do in making the sale in the first place.

Special Note: On the following pages, you'll hear from Ari Galper. Ari is a specialist in creating exceptionally sophisticated, precision language sales presentations and conversations that not only improve sales results but also create and strengthen relationships. Ari is a member of my Platinum Private Client Group and has been of valuable assistance to many of my clients in structuring more effective sales presentations, and improving conversions at their marketing and e-commerce websites with "live" dialogue with visitors, using his ChatWise® technology. While Ari and I are not in 100% agreement in our approaches to selling—and, if we agreed on everything, one of us would be unnecessary—we are in sync on the need for more professional and thoughtful selling in The New Economy. I believe you'll find his perspective on this provocative.

Discover Why Creating Trust Is the Secret to Generating New Sales Opportunities in The New Economy

By Ari Galper, Creator of Unlock The Game®

If you flick through the pages of business magazines and traditional sales training material, you will find a constant flow of messages like, "Focus on closing the sale"; "Overcome objections"; "Be relentless"; "Accept rejection as a normal part of selling"; and "Chase the sale."

In most cases, it becomes about getting the sale at the expense of the human relationship. For the customer, this approach is transparent and all too familiar. But in this New Economy, there is a much better way to succeed in selling. It begins with moving away from the hidden agenda of focusing on making the sale. When you do this, a new world opens up for you. In other words, when you stop just selling and start building authentic relationships based on trust, authenticity, and integrity, the possibilities become endless. It's a whole new mind-set in selling, which I call Unlock The Game®.

The vast majority of traditional sales techniques contradict everything we know about what it takes to build relationships. But shouldn't selling be about creating new relationships with customers, clients, and patients? No one likes to be pushed and no one wants to talk to someone whose only agenda is to get what they want.

Have you ever made a sale without trying to "make the sale"? You know what I mean, it just happened naturally without you having to force it to happen. That process you did unconsciously is the process that I have created at the conscious level so that you have **a "system" you can follow** that makes the sales process effortless.

Selling is all about trust. People can sense when you are more concerned about your commission than their best interests. When you treat people as people, not prospects, and reveal your trustworthiness, they will start to trust you. They will see you as a problem solver focused solely on their needs. From there you have the basis of a long-term relationship—the true competitive advantage in this New Economy.

New Mind-Set + New Results

If you've only been exposed to one way of selling, then this chart will give you a quick comparison to see where you're current sales mind-set is and what areas of your mind-set may need to shift to get the results you're looking for.

Mind-Set Chart

Old Sales Mind-Set	New Sales Mind-Set
Always start out with a strong sales pitch.	Hold the sales pitch. Start a conversation.
Your goal is always to close the sale.	Your goal is always to discover whether you and your prospect are a good fit. Then close the sale "naturally."
When you lose a sale, it's usually at the end of the sales process.	When you lose a sale, it's usually at the beginning of the sales process.
Keep chasing prospects until you get a yes or no.	Never chase prospects. Instead, get to the truth of whether there's a fit or not.
When prospects offer objections, challenge and/or counter them.	When prospects offer objections, validate them and reopen the conversation.
If prospects challenge the value of your product or service, defend yourself and explain its value.	Never defend yourself or what you have to offer. This only creates more sales pressure.

Let's take a closer look at these concepts so you can begin to open up your current sales thinking and become more effective in your selling efforts.

1. Stop the sales pitch. Start a conversation.

When you begin talking with your prospect, never start out with a mini-presentation about yourself, your company, and what you have to offer.

Instead, start with a conversational phrase that focuses on a specific problem that your product or service solves. For example, you might say, "I'm just calling to see if you are open to some different ideas related to preventing downtime across your computer network?"

Notice that you're not pitching your solution with this opening phrase. Instead, you're addressing a problem that, based on your experience in your field, you believe they might be having. (If you don't know what problems your product or service solves, do a little research by asking your current customers why they purchased your solution.)

2. Your goal is always to discover whether you and your prospect are a good fit.

By simply focusing your conversation on problems that you can help prospects solve, and by not jumping the gun by trying to move the sales process forward, you'll discover that prospects will give you the direction you need.

3. When you lose a sale, it's usually at the beginning of the sales process.

If you think you're losing sales due to mistakes you make at the end of the process, review how you began the relationship. Did you start with a pitch?

Did you use traditional sales language ("We have a solution that you really need" or "Others in your industry have bought our solution, you should consider it as well")?

Traditional sales language leads prospects to label you with the negative stereotype of "salesperson." This makes it almost impossible for them to relate to you with trust or to have an honest, open conversation about problems they're trying to solve and how you might be able to help them. As Dan said, the last thing you want to be is "another salesperson."

4. Never chase prospects. Instead, get to the truth of whether there's a fit or not.

Chasing prospects has always been considered normal and necessary, but it's rooted in the macho selling image that "If you don't keep chasing, you're giving up, which means you're a failure." This is dead wrong.

Instead, ask your prospects if they'd be open to connecting again at a certain time and date so you can both avoid the phone tag game. Further, if you play the game better, prospects will chase you.

5. When prospects offer objections, validate them, and reopen the conversation.

Most traditional sales programs spend a lot of time focusing on "overcoming" objections, but these tactics only create more sales pressure.

They also keep you from exploring or learning the truth behind what your prospects are saying.

You know that "We don't have the budget," "Send me information," or "Call me back in a few months" are polite evasions designed to get you off the phone. Stop trying to counter objections. Instead, shift to uncovering the truth by replying, "That's not a problem." No matter what the objection, use gentle, dignified language that invites prospects to tell you the truth about their situation without feeling you'll use it to press for a sale.

6. Never defend yourself or what you have to offer. This only creates more sales pressure.

When prospects say, "Why should I choose you over your competition?" your instinctive reaction is to defend your product or service because you believe that you are the best choice, and you want to convince them of that. But what goes through their minds at that point?

Something like, "This 'salesperson' is trying to sell me, and I hate feeling as if I'm being sold."

Stop defending yourself. In fact, come right out and tell them that you aren't going to try to convince them of anything because that only creates sales pressure. Instead, ask them again about key problems they're trying to solve.

Then explore how your product or service might solve those problems. Give up trying to persuade. Let prospects feel they can choose you without feeling sold.

The sooner you can begin to shift your mind-set toward creating trust with your prospects, the sooner you can start bringing in more sales and creating long-term relationships.

Ari Galper is creator of Unlock The Game®, a new sales mind-set and approach that overturns the notion of selling as we know it today. Ari has over a decade of experience creating breakthrough sales strategies for global companies such as UPS and QUALCOMM. Ari discovered the missing link that people who sell have been seeking for years. His profound discovery of shifting one's mind-set to a place of complete integrity, based on new words and phrases grounded in sincerity, has earned him distinction as the world's leading authority on how to build trust in the world of selling. He also has completely redefined how to connect with people over the phone. In his corporate training sessions, Ari demonstrates his mind-set by calling new prospects in front of live audiences. These strategies have led to his Chatwise® technology that changes the game for online/internet marketers.

Unlock the Game® has over 30,000 clients, members and sub-scribers along with sales professionals from the following companies: Motorola, Gateway, Clear Channel Communications, Brother International, Fidelity National Mortgage, ERA, Pitney Bowes, The NPD Group, AFLAC, State Farm Insurance, Coldwell Banker, Radisson Hotels, AON Consulting, Pre-Paid Legal, Telecom Plus, Century 21 Realty, Executive Search Group, RE/MAX, and Realty Executives.

You can take a Free Test Drive of Unlock The Game® at www.UnlockTheGame.com or get a Free 15-Minute Sales Script Review by calling 866-530-5125.

PART IV

DUMB AND DUMBER
THINGS THAT SABOTAGE
SALES SUCCESS

CHAPTER 19

B.S. THAT
SALES MANAGERS SHOVEL
ONTO SALESPEOPLE

Bluntly, a lot of sales managers aren't parked behind the big desk bellowing at you because they deserve to be there.

Some are sales burn-outs, promoted to get them out of the field. Some were top salespeople, now promoted per the Peter Principle to their level of incompetence. Some are woefully lazy. Many are stubborn and close-minded, stuck in whatever era they were in at their peak. Like the 1950s. Just as the leading cause of death is hospitalization, the prime cause of a lot of sales career death is the sales manager!

Here are the dumbest things I catch such sales managers telling their troops:

1. "The Answer to Your Problem Is Simple: Make More Calls."

No, that's not the answer. If you are not being effective at setting appointments, increasing the quantity of ineffective calls only speeds up the pace of failure. If you drink a sip of spoiled milk and feel nauseous, gulping down the rest of the carton isn't the cure.

Ignore this simple-minded advice and refer, instead, to Chapter 17. Implement a system that gets more good prospects calling you.

"We just haven't been flapping them hard enough."

2. "Everybody's Your Prospect."

No, they are not. When everybody's a theoretical prospect, nobody's a real prospect. Before The New Economy, salespeople could still earn a living with this 1950's approach—even though the fragmentation of the market, the importance of specialization, and the insistence by consumers on specific relevance to them was well underway. These are not sudden trends. But they are now dominant. New Economy Customers are quicker than ever to effectively slam the door in the face of any salesperson trying to peddle the same dog food to every dog owner, regardless of breed, size, or age of their pups. You need a clear, in-depth profile of your ideal customer, and you then need to devise a system for attracting those customers—and preferably just those customers—to you.

Refer to Chapter 17.

3. "It Is Easier to Sell to Someone Who Isn't Interested than It Is to Find Someone Who Is."

It may be easier to get sex by taking a big club, whacking an unsuspecting woman over the head, dragging her back to your cave, and having your way with her than to meet, repeatedly date, get to know, build trust with, and seduce her, but it's an antiquated, primitive—and illegal—approach. Similarly, brute force selling to the uninterested is a primitive, ugly approach. Antiquated, and even rapidly becoming illegal. Hopefully you are well aware, we now live in the age of the Do Not Call List, laws restricting use of broadcast fax and broadcast voice (robocalling), anti-spam laws, and even pending legislation to govern unwanted mail. The "No Solicitors" signs are proliferating.

Further, forcing yourself on someone who isn't ideally matched with what you sell and isn't interested in and motivated by what you sell may be a way to grind out a living from commission checks, but it's no way to build a sustainable, secure, and exceptionally successful career. Even more importantly, it's a guarantee of future burn-out, fatigue, dissatisfaction, cynicism. The stress of forcing people to buy things they aren't eager to buy and own is wearing. This is just no way to go through life. And anyone advising you to go through life this way certainly does not have your best interests in mind—and is probably ignorant about marketing.

The New Economy outright *demands* a higher level of sophistication from successful sales professionals. Advertising, marketing, and selling can no longer be separated as if three different functions rather than the seamless process it should be. And my strongest advice to you is to educate yourself not just about selling, but to become a smart, skilled marketing professional and to take control of a marketing process that brings you ideally suited prospects eager to meet with you, respectful of your expertise and advice, and a pleasure to deal with.

I have a saying, something I constantly talk with my clients about: it's not just the money you make, it's how you make the money. Life is too short *and* life is too long to spend it hi-ho, hi-ho, it's off to work we go. Selling should not be drudgery.

4. "Your Problem Is You're Not Motivated."

My entire no-prospecting, "Magnetic Marketing" approach grew out of frustration with motivation. I had the car seat full of motivational tapes but I still had an empty bank account. The world's greatest attitude is no better than the world's worst attitude if you aren't sitting across from a highly qualified, able-to-buy prospect. Motivation is fine, motivational influences and influencers have their place, self-motivation is best, but the key to it all isn't pumping yourself up or being pumped up with pep talks; the key is having reasons to expect positive results. If you put in place the strategies and practices described in this book and go beyond them, to being a full-scale marketing professional, you won't need to "get motivated." You'll *be* motivated, with good reason.

With #3 and #4 here in mind, I must insert a commercial. There are a few additional books of mine I want to urge reading, and a collection of free resources I want you to have, to guide you in quick move up from sales professional to marketing professional. The *No B.S. Guide to Direct Marketing* gives you a quick, concise fast start in using smart marketing in place of manual labor to attract, interest, develop and prepare prospects to become great customers by their choice rather than your force. It includes actual examples and even marketing samples from a number of sales professionals-turned-marketing professionals. The *NO B.S. Guide to Time Management* is about more; it is about autonomy, about making money in a way that pleases you and is respectful of you. In addition, I'd like you to experience two months of Glazer-Kennedy Insider's Circle™ Membership free of fee, including my *No B.S. Marketing Letter,* Marketing Gold Audio CD's, webinars, and more. You'll find that offer on pages 260–261 or go directly to www.FreeGiftFrom.com.sales.

Free Gift Offer

Get Dan's Greatest FREE GIFT Offer at www.FreeGift From.com.sales. Get more information about all of Dan's books and see video-presentations at www.NoBSBooks.com.

5. "It's Just a Numbers Game. Keep at It."

OK, there's some truth to this. But—and it's a big "but" (just like the sales manager's!)—just stepping up to the plate and taking more swings, if you can't hit, won't help. It is, in part, a numbers game. But it's also a game of strategy and skill. You want to be persistent, but you want to apply that persistence as productively as possible. As I said much earlier in this book, most sales pros— even doing everything brilliantly—are still going to hear a lot of No's, Maybe's, and Maybe Later's. Selling is not the right profession for the individual weak of will or short of stamina. There's much to be said for keeping at it, as long as that "it" is carefully chosen.

How to Tell a Good Sales Manager from a Bad One

A good sales manager teaches strategy, coaches skills, and works with you to solve problems and manage your opportunities. He does NOT regurgitate any of the above five B.S. clichés. He understands and supports sophisticated lead generation and prequalifying efforts, to make your time more productive. In fact, he is a serious student of marketing and direct marketing, not just sales. So, a word to any sales manager reading this, including those I've offended: it's past time for you to reinvent yourself, your know-how and tool kit, your modus operandi for success in The New Economy. You can be an enormous asset to your company and greatly improve the productivity of your sales force by bringing direct marketing in, to replace old-fashioned prospecting, so your salespeople spend more time selling to people primed to buy. Check out the same resources I suggested above.

A bad sales manager spits out the above five B.S. clichés so frequently and repeatedly it's as if he has one of those pull-strings in his back, and a computer chip for a brain. Saddled with such, you have only two choices: ignore him, or get away from him and go and find a better opportunity.

CHAPTER 20

SIX DUMBEST THINGS
SALESPEOPLE DO TO
SABOTAGE THEMSELVES

Most salespeople I know cut their own income by at least 75%, with no help needed from dysfunctional sales managers, corporate home office pinheads, tough competition, troubles in the economy, or meddling in their field by politicians. They are their own worst enemies.

For too long, the economy was forgiving of these sins, and salespeople guilty of some or even all of them could still do well. I am absolutely delighted that is no longer the case. As the recession revealed the slop and sloth and miserable disservice run rampant in many businesses, large and small, and wiped many off the landscape, I celebrated their demise. As quite a few salespeople stumbled from unearned prosperity to shock and starvation, I thanked the recession for its overdue good work. Now The

New Economy will provide greater rewards than ever to those who step up, and will go right on meting out harsher punishments than ever for those who won't. Here are six poor behaviors that will make you deservedly poor should you persist in them in The New Economy:

1. Lousy Follow-Up

If you've ever gone to a trade show as a buyer, as I do, you know that you will get follow-up from nearly none of the salespeople you talk to in the booth. You might, might get sent the same dumb brochure you were handed at the booth. That's it. This pathetic situation actually permeates leads produced from all sources. Most salespeople under-value leads, have no follow-up SYSTEM in place, and rarely exhibit any persistence in following up on leads.

Most of the successful clients I work with or who are in my coaching programs have 8 to 28 steps in their prospect follow-up sequences, which may include multiple mailings, e-mail, fax, invitations to lunches, seminars, teleseminars, online "webinars," and more. For example, a client, a salesman of a $20,000.00 business product, has gone from $200,000.00 to $500,000.00 a year in commissions in the past 24 months by, at my urging, adding five follow-up steps beyond his norm; three lengthy letters two weeks apart, followed by a faxed invitation to a group teleseminar held only for these unconverted leads. He closes as many sales from these added five steps as from his regular selling activity.

2. Hanging Out with Losers

In virtually every sales organization, 5% make 95% of the money. If you are wasting your time hanging around 95%'ers, you get crumbs.

Toxic influences are less affordable than ever. You need to be mentally sharp. Hanging around with anybody not all about success; hanging out with the lazy, the un-curious, the complainers and whiners, the complacent has to get to zero. Find and associate *only* with winners.

3. Hanging Out with the Losers at the Bar, Strip Club, or Coffee Shop

No additional commentary needed.

4. Wasting Time

Walk into the typical auto showroom, pool and patio store, or some other business where customers come to the salespeople. Watch everybody. Most of the salespeople are standing around waiting, talking to each other, munching doughnuts, and drinking coffee. They're playing games on their computers, texting their friends. Not selling. The two car sales guys I know, who each earn over $200,000.00 a year, never take a walk-in, never stand around waiting for a turn. They are busy with appointments, generated proactively.

Bill Glazer, President of Glazer-Kennedy Insider's Circle™, which publishes my *No B.S. Marketing Letter,* is a marketing coach to retail store owners, and also, up until very recently leaving that business by choice, owned two thriving menswear stores in Baltimore. He made sure his in-store clothing salespeople did well over 40% of their business by pre-set appointments with their customers. When they weren't engaged in selling, they were mailing or calling their clients to set up appointments, not standing around sucking up java. That's what coffee breaks are for.

5. Not Creating SYSTEMS

The seat-of-the-pants salesperson will never, ever match the income of the systemized salesperson. The top producers live by systems.

They have a system for generating a steady stream of good leads from multiple sources. They have an intake system for those leads, for categorizing them, managing them, following up on them with multiple steps and multiple types of media. If the system, for example, calls for four letters, each seven days apart, by God, each prospect gets each letter on schedule. Top performers also have a system for selling. My own "million dollar presentation" I use from the platform, the process and language I use in selling my consulting and copywriting services, all scripted, rehearsed, fine-tuned, and memorized. I subscribe to David Sandler's axiom: if you do not have a system for selling, you are at the mercy of the prospect's system for buying (or not buying).

Finally, top performers have an organized, multi-step system for encouraging, obtaining, and rewarding referrals.

Think about this: most businesses and companies have very detailed *operating* systems. But most have random and erratic acts of selling. I suppose by nature, or by habit, most salespeople chafe at rules, standards, set procedures, structured presentations, structured work—and that's one of the chief reasons there is such a huge disparity in income between the 95% group and the elite 5% in every sales organization. If you really want to be in the 5%, you will impose your own structures.

A good way of looking at this, suggested to business owners by Michael Gerber, author of *The E-Myth*: organize your business into systems so it could be franchised like McDonalds, even if you have no intention of ever doing so. I would suggest the very same idea to the sales professional. In fact, you need to manage yourself as your employee, and your selling as your business. For that purpose, read my book, *No B.S. Guide to Ruthless Management of People and Profits*.

6. Poor Self-Discipline

For several years, I was on about 20 programs a year as a speaker with General Norman Schwarzkopf immediately preceding me. Norm echoed some classic advice to military men and women: the difference between a live soldier and a dead one is discipline.

Top salespeople hold themselves accountable. They organize each week's and day's work, they have goals and standards and benchmarks, they get going early in the morning and they keep going all day.

PART V

MY BIGGEST SECRET
TO EXCEPTIONAL RESULTS IN SELLING:
TAKEAWAY SELLING

CHAPTER 21

THE AWESOME POWER
OF TAKEAWAY SELLING

I n this chapter of the book, I reveal THE secret that I have relied on most heavily in the last 20 years, during which my personal earnings skyrocketed, along with my prominence in the fields in which I work.

Proving the Theory of Supply and Demand

In many ways, Takeaway Selling contradicts classic wisdom about selling. One of the most important underlying principles behind Takeaway Selling is the law of supply and demand and how it affects people's desires. As a rule of thumb, the less accessible something is, the greater the value that gets placed on it and the more people who want it. And my whole approach to selling is to sell what the customer wants and spend my time only selling to customers who want what I sell. Tilting the reality or at least their perception of supply-demand in my favor is key.

I spent too many years of my adult life dead broke, and that was a mystery to me for quite awhile. I had my dog-eared copy of *Think and Grow Rich,* kept a car seat full of motivational tapes, went to seminars, faced the mirror and said my positive affirmations out loud every morning, tried hypnosis, subliminals, and every other darned thing, and I had some pretty sharp skills. And I was still walking around with a big, blustery smile on my face with nothing but hungry moths in my wallet. Finally, I determined that the missing link to success is mastering supply and demand because as soon as there is, consistently, a greater demand for your services than there is supply of your time, it's ridiculously easy to be successful.

There is no more powerful force than supply and demand. It is behind virtually every war. It controls and regulates price of virtually every commodity, from the corn you buy at the supermarket to the gasoline you put into your car, as well as to commodities cleverly decommoditized, like diamonds, Beanie Babies,̊ and limited edition this or that. It emboldens or weakens every provider of any service, permitting some to selectively choose their clientele and charge top fees, while causing others providing that very same service to accept anybody with a pulse as a client—even when convinced in advance the relationship will go badly—and to grovel when quoting their low prices. About this, you'll find an interview with "the $250,000.00 portrait photographer" at the end of this chapter, reprinted from my *No B.S. Marketing to the Affluent Letter*, one of the Glazer-Kennedy Insider's Circle™ newsletters. **Lifting the lid from your earnings and earning your income much more pleasantly is directly connected to your mastery of supply and demand.**

In my businesses, as a consultant, copywriter, and speaker, I've learned that **demand definitely breeds demand**. The busier I am, the more people want my services; the less accessible I am, the more I'm appreciated; the less the supply of me, the greater the demand—and the virtual absence of fee resistance. That's one of the reasons I sometimes publish a frequently updated, detailed copy of my schedule. I send it to clients and prospective clients, and when they see the supply-demand ratio, they act.

These days, this technique is 100% legitimate; I really am overbooked and it is a struggle to fit in new clients, projects, and engagements. But I'll frankly tell you that I did my best to create this appearance and foster this image before it was a total reality. For example, even when I'm in the office, I very, very rarely take an incoming call from anybody and that's been my policy for years—years before it was a time management necessity. Often to even have a phone conversation with me, it has to be scheduled as an appointment a week to several weeks in advance.

I also haven't used business cards in years. At speaking engagements, there are always a few people who do not rush to purchase the materials I offer but instead come to me asking for my business card. I tell them that I don't believe in them, and I tell them why: if they aren't interested enough in what I've talked about there to invest a couple of hundred dollars, why would I want them calling me at my office? When new prospects call my office, they're usually advised to send a brief memo to my attention, describing what they wish to discuss with me, then my assistant will get back to them and arrange a telephone appointment for them to speak with me. Again, these are now time management necessities. But I implemented them for their sales impact before they became unavoidable.

I describe all this in detail in my *No B.S. Time Management for Entrepreneurs* book. Typically, sales professionals of almost every stripe at first insist they can't follow my model in their business, that their clients would never sit still for such limited and rationed access, and that making prospects wait and "jump through hoops" for access will send them to competitors. But I can prove—and do prove—that the exact opposite is true. Over years, countless initially skeptical and nervous sales professionals have become converts, and their incomes are higher and lives better for it.

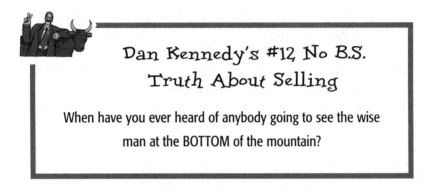

Dan Kennedy's #12 No B.S. Truth About Selling

When have you ever heard of anybody going to see the wise man at the BOTTOM of the mountain?

How a Starving Dog Trainer Rid Her Finances of Fleas, Once and For All

At a seminar I was speaking at, Elizabeth R. cornered me on a break to tell me her troubles. She was a very talented, very capable dog obedience trainer. Her credentials, references, and testimonials were pretty impressive. She had a jazzy brochure. She resided in a high-income area. But she was having a devil of a time making ends meet. "What do you charge?" I asked. "$20.00 an hour," she answered—and she went to the customers' homes to train their dogs.

I told her, "You are a professional—a dog therapist. Triple your fee, make the client bring the dog to you, and do not even agree to accept a new client's dog until the dog takes your special IQ test for dogs. Charge a fee for the initial client consultation and test the dog to be sure it has enough basic intelligence and the proper attitude to respond to training. And make each new client wait at least a week before you fit him or her in."

"Immediately send a letter to all your past clients, thanking them for all their past referrals but advising them that, because of the overwhelming demand, you have no choice but to impose new restrictions on accepting new clients. Send a similar letter to present clients, but offer them services at your old fees for six more months. Stop answering your own phone. Dress better."

This kind of move takes guts. When you are sitting there, twiddling your thumbs and worrying about the checkbook balance, it requires a lot of nerve *not* to grab that phone yourself on the first ring, jump in, and sell, sell, sell. I know, I've been there.

A few months after the seminar Elizabeth dropped me a note, letting me know she'd had her first $10,000.00 month, and felt certain she'd make more than $100,000.00 in the next year.

Interestingly, the Barkley Pet Hotel and Spa, where we now board our "Million Dollar Dog"—her title, not her name; that's Lady—requires new dogs to have a psychological and behavioral assessment before being permitted to participate in group play and doggie day camp while staying there. The Million Dollar Dog flunked, by the way; influenced by me, she is too territorial and does not play well with others, so she must have private play times (at added cost). The Barkley also provides dog training if desired, walks and limo rides, belly rub time, even bedtime stories. Three different size suites, dining options, grooming, and more. A new client must attend a tour and orientation offered only at certain times before being accepted and being able to board a dog there. I was way ahead of them in dispensing my advice to Elizabeth back in 1994. Now I'm a "victim" of my own advice!

A Real Estate Agent to Learn From

Real estate agent Peggy B. gets 70% of her listings from referrals, 30% from advertising. Either way, when someone interested in listing a home with Peggy calls her office, the receptionist transfers the call to one of Peggy's three assistants. The assistant explains that, because Peggy's services are so much in demand, she employs three client service specialists to, among other things, screen her calls and make certain that the caller's property meets the strict criteria Peggy has for her listings—otherwise the caller will be referred to another agent.

The assistant then asks the caller a dozen questions, completing a form as she goes. Ultimately, an appointment is set for Peggy to visit the client's home several days later.

Next, a DVD "documentary" about Peggy, her unusual success, and the thorough services she provides is delivered by messenger to the caller's home. The assistant calls the day of the appointment to be certain that both husband and wife have watched the DVD. In the rare instance where they have not, the assistant postpones or cancels the appointment.

At the appointment time, the assistant, not Peggy, arrives at the home. She bears a gift of a little package of cookies from a local, upscale bakery, and the bad news that Peggy will be delayed by no more than 20 minutes at a closing. In the meantime, the assistant provides information on the recent selling prices of comparable nearby homes, the length of times they've been on the market, related data, and how that is used to calculate a reasonable range from which Peggy will determine their best listing price. Peggy tells me it's better to have this "dirty work" done by the assistant before she arrives, giving the client time to think about those numbers versus their all-too-often unrealistic expectations concerning the price.

About 15 minutes later, Peggy calls from her cell phone to announce her imminent arrival. Minutes later, in one of her bright-colored, gold ornament-trimmed Cadillacs, Peggy arrives.

After apologies and pleasantries, she listens as her assistant quickly "briefs" her, summarizing what's been discussed so far and setting up the price range. Next, Peggy asks if, while they talk, it's okay if her assistant goes through the house and takes photographs for potential use in advertising, brochures, websites, and displays at the office. (This, in case you don't recognize it, is a trial close. Why would they let her go ahead with photography if they weren't going to list the house with Peggy?)

The assistant takes her top-quality camera and goes about her business, while Peggy uses her "flip book" to explain the ten steps they'll use together to get the best possible price for the home in the shortest possible time. At the end, there's a listing agreement, already partially completed by the assistant from the information obtained over the phone.

Last year, Peggy listed 92% of the homes where she made this listing presentation immediately, without delay. In almost every one of those cases, Peggy charged an "advertising cost" to the client and collected that from the new client on the spot, too—something most agents do not do. And, of the 8% she did not get immediately, half came to her later.

"What happens," I asked Peggy, "when the client objects to that charge, or the price you want them to set, or they question whether or not you'll be able to give their property's sale enough attention, considering how busy you are?"

She replied: "It rarely happens because of the way our relationship is set up from the beginning. But when it does, I TAKE IT AWAY from them. I'll say something like 'Well, different approaches are right for different people. You may be more comfortable with a more conventional agent, somebody who will sit here day after day on open houses, be around the office whenever you call, and not be so selective about taking clients.' Then I'll pull out my address book and start to recommend a couple of 'those kinds' of agents. The client invariably back pedals."

I first met Peggy years ago, and included her in prior editions of this book; I checked, and she's still doing business pretty much the same way. And other leaders in this field—notably a client of mine, Craig Proctor, consistently one of the top ten RE/MAX agents in the world, and a top business coach to more than 3,000 other agents—conducts his business in much the same way. And yes, even in a "tough market." Actually, Takeaway Selling was even more important in down markets.

The Power of "Disqualification"

Most salespeople complain about having too few leads, and struggle mightily to get the ones they get. The sales professionals using all my "Magnetic Marketing" methods attract more leads than they can handle. This supports a radical shift in thinking, to disqualifying prospects as quickly as possible. When you have plenty of choices about who to invest time in, you only want to invest it in what I call Highest Probability Prospects, getting rid of the others, fast. Ruthlessly.

A number of years back, through a sequence of unusual circumstances, I wound up majority stockholder in and CEO of a custom manufacturing company in a tiny niche. This company was losing money at a breakneck pace, had every business problem imaginable and few unimaginable ones, and as it had no cash, I was not only CEO, but also Vice-Presidents, plural, of everything, and National Sales Manager. After about a month as Sales Manager, I made an astounding discovery: we were manufacturing a lot more quotes than anything else. Our two sales reps were spending half their time doing quotes. We were a quote machine. Unfortunately, only 20% of the clients getting quotes provided were converting, and of those, it was taking an average of five different quotes to wind up with one order. There was a lot of "quote it again with blue boxes instead of four-color" sort of activity.

To the screaming anguish of the sales reps, I instituted a new policy: $500.00 charged any new, prospective client for quotes on a project, $200.00 to all but a few "Grade AAA" established clients, applied to the order but otherwise non-refundable, paid in advance, credit card or check. For about two weeks, the reps alternated the death march in and out of my office, weeping, wailing, and gnashing their teeth over all the prospects who were outraged and going elsewhere for quotes. However, at the end of 60 days, the results told a different story. We now issued about one-third fewer new project quotes, and had driven off only 18 of about 300 past accounts, all 18 high in the pain-in-rear quotient, low in profit. Conversions on the two-thirds new project quotes done doubled. The speed of the process, quote to conversion, went from an average of 40 days to 15, thanks to another of my new policies: quote fee refundable only for 21 days. Further, overall sales were up because the reps had more time to sell, to follow-up (only) on really viable leads, had less activity swirling around them thus a clearer, more harshly accurate picture of what might close in the immediate future. One of the two, who actually "got it," tripled her commissions over the next three months. By forcing her to disqualify, I multiplied her income.

Being aggressive about disqualifying a prospect takes courage. Being a sales wimp, though, carries its own high price in pain.

How Do New Economy Customers Respond to Takeaway Selling?

When it's done right—_better than ever._

The New Economy Customer are, as I've repeatedly emphasized, more discerning, more circumspect, more critically analytical. They are in search of trustworthy expertise, not just products and services, in virtually every category. They want the best value for their money, not necessarily the lowest price or fee. Consequently, they are assessing and judging the sales professionals they encounter, they sift and sort and choose in new and different ways. They are willing to wait, even to qualify for the opportunity to work with the best, the most competent, the most expert real estate agent, financial advisor, pest control operator, even dog trainer.

For you, there's a second incentive to master and convert to Takeaway Selling: power. In The New Economy, the power shifted back to the customers and they're well aware of it. In order to recapture power in the buying-selling equation, you need to be dealing with prospects and customers especially eager and pre-disposed to be doing business only with you. It may be counter-intuitive, but the reality is that you can't get into that position with traditional selling approaches. You can't get into that positioning by being more accessible, more instantly and continuously accessible, overly eager, too "easy" to every and any suitor. Once a relationship is in place, of course, providing exceptional service as agreed to by you and your customers is crucial. At the very first point of entry, such as via your lead generation advertising, walking through a door and identifying themselves as valid prospects needs to be easy. But in between that first step and an actual relationship, you can only gain and own power by making the customer earn the opportunity to be accepted as your customer or client.

A Fundamental Choice

Whether you use Takeaway Selling or not is a fundamental choice about how you are going to go through your career, what kind of experience it is going to be for you and for your customers or clients. Takeaway Selling actually is win-win. Clients feel good about being privileged, being special, being in an elite group, and if they get that feeling by doing business with you, then you are providing significant added value. You will have much more energy and enthusiasm, bring more creativity to your clients' needs, and derive greater satisfaction from your daily experience if you are dealing with people who do feel privileged dealing with you!

A Picture Is Worth a Thousand Words, and $237,000.00

In lieu of a Field Trip and a Copywriting Corner this month, I instead bring you my complete interview with "the $250,000.00 photographer"—and then suggest your own field trip to his website.

JOHN ZEULI photographs industry icons including a number of Forbes 400 CEOs and entrepreneurs, political leaders, authors, artists and other high profile individuals. That list includes Erin Brokovich, Bryan Moss (former chairman, Gulfstream), Robert Redford, Ellyn Burstyn, George Foreman, authors Patricia Cornwell, Pat Conroy, Paula Deen. His most elite program, "Legacy," requires a $237,000.00 fee. An individual's Legacy Exhibit includes the photography; 15 archival, museum-quality, framed prints; 7 handcrafted books featuring the photographs; a digital slide show; and high resolution digital file of all the photographs. Some clients invest in excess of $250,000.00. He has offered to photograph The Million Dollar Dog, which would risk making her title literally accurate. He is based on Savannah, Georgia, the locale featured in the novel and movie *Midnight in the Garden of Good and Evil*, and provides a "Savannah experience" as one option for clients. You may look at John's business at: www.JohnZeuliPhotography.com.

His connection to me, from John: "I have studied your material off and on for years. I do much better financially when I have you in the 'on' position! Twenty some years ago I owned a jewelry store and I remember selling over $60,000.00 in one day using one of your strategies—and $60,000.00 was a lot back then. No doubt you saw your influence throughout my literature."

The Interview . . .

DAN: I wonder about your advertised and imposed limitation of only working with seven individuals a year—and I'm considering such a thing for myself . . . and of the category exclusivity you offer, only working with one individual in a given industry or profession. What leaps out of your material is what I call "manufactured differentiation." I'd like you to comment on when and how you developed this position and why you find it persuasive with your clientele.

JOHN: Only working with seven clients per year at the Legacy Level, and only one per industry or profession, is a very deliberate exclusivity-differentiation. My experience is that extremely successful and high-profile individuals are competitive. They are keenly aware of what their peers are up to. They want to be first. Exclusive, special.

DAN: If alert, people just got their price of admission to this interview back in spades in one sentence in that answer—it should leap out. The fees also leap out! Your Legacy package carries a $237,000.00 price tag. A lesser package is also offered at $57,000.00. The cynics might guess the $237,000.00 a red herring, to make $57,000.00 seem reasonable and attractive, and I hope you don't mind me asking abut that. With either fee, most will assume your clientele is limited to only the Very Rich; what I identify in my *Marketing to the Affluent* book as ULTRA-Affluent, and your prospective clients to be very limited in number. True or false? I'm guessing neither to be true—that your clientele comes from a broader range of affluence. Tell us what you're willing to share about the types of clients you work with.

JOHN: I am certainly expensive. Yes, the $237K makes the $57K seem affordable and reasonable, however the more expensive package is not a red herring—in the sense that this is where my future lies. When I authentically put it out there, I get response; if I never put it out there, it would never happen. My client base tends to start at affluent and go up to ultra-affluent. Not surprisingly, the more affluent the clients are, the easier and more fun they are to work with. If I lower my fee to help someone afford me, I inevitably "get bitten in the butt"—I encourage my wife to remind me to "just say no!" If I encounter someone solely price conscious, I refer them to another photographer. Better they go crazy than me.

DAN: From a marketing standpoint, how did you build your business and your reputation? Were there big breakthroughs that catapulted you to this level? How have you secured these clients before you had many to provide referrals?

JOHN: From studying your work, and from hard knocks, I realized that waiting to be discovered OR climbing up some ladder was a fool's game. I used the express elevator to the top. For my business, high-profile individuals are the express elevator. I declared myself to be a high-profile photographer and sought out this niche. Initially, I approached high-profile people to be photographed for certain portrait exhibits. I did not charge. Before long they were referring peers to me who paid. And, as I featured more high-profile people on my website, other "regular" clients expected to pay more.

DAN: As they say in the Guinness commercials, brilliant! The "created reason" to get to exactly the people you want to get to, without asking for business and clients out of the gate, is readily available in some variation to everybody, yet so few use it. Years ago, I counseled a management/leadership trainer and consultant who wanted to build a local practice with corporations in his home city, to contact the 100 top CEO's, to interview them for his forthcoming book on leadership. He easily entered doors that would otherwise have

stayed sealed shut, he spent 30 to 90 minutes with each CEO, mostly listening, and it will be no surprise to you that his entire business was almost instantly built.

It is obvious you don't "sell pictures." At least, I hope it's obvious. So many make less than they could and struggle unnecessarily simply "things." How would you describe what you do—and what your clients feel they are buying?

JOHN: You are correct; I do NOT sell pictures, and I feel strongly about this. If that's all they want, I'd rather they go elsewhere. Rather, I create extremely positive experiences and memories for individuals, couples, families, and organizations. While providing stellar images is critical, on many levels it is still an addendum to the experience. Through the experiences and resulting poignant images created, I've helped strengthen, nurture, and even heal relationships. This puts the fee in perspective, by the way—after all, what does a divorce cost? Being a catalyst to improving relationships is significant and priceless work, and frankly, I need to articulate this better in my literature.

DAN: Your end comment demonstrates the importance of constantly re-thinking our businesses, re-evaluating positioning and presentations, and finding opportunities to be prodded by people who "get it" . . . my plug for participation in local Glazer-Kennedy Chapters, the Peak Performers group, coming to events. Back to the actual question, I think your firm position on not wanting people of a certain frame of mind about this as clients is very significant.

As a final question, everybody will wonder about the impact of the economic mess on your business. Is there impact? Is it causing you to alter any marketing, pricing, or other aspect of your business?

JOHN: Yes, I've noticed impact with the economic downturn. While the ultra-affluent are still rich by my and by most standards, it's all relative, subject to individual perception. If they *feel* fearful, they become cautious. Competition also matters more, and my competitors are not other photographers, but the other luxuries they might consider. My job, heightened at this time, is to convince them to purchase what I offer rather than a new luxury auto or another trip through Europe. If I'm changing anything, it's in the search. There's a sentence in one of Frank Herbert's *Dune* novels: "Fortune changes hands in times of crisis." My job is to find the new hands.

CHAPTER 22

A Final Word
from the Author

Over 30+ years I've heard and participated in a **great deal of talk about what "selling" is.** To some, it's just a job, in some cases, something temporary. Actor-producer Tom Selleck sold menswear. There's no telling how many unemployed actors have sold the famous Cutco® knives. One of the most famous motivational speakers of all time, my speaking colleague of a decade, Zig Ziglar, sold cookware, door to door. To many it becomes their lifetime career, some staying in and excelling in one field, others moving from industry to industry, as trends change or new opportunities present themselves. To some small percentage of those, it becomes a profession, and they treat it with appropriate respect and dedication. To many, it is the means of starting a business that grows into a company, even into a global empire, as with Mary Kay or Rich DeVos and Jay Van Andel, who founded Amway after stints as door-to-door distributors in another company, or W. Clement Stone in insurance, or me. A great many of the business empires putting the richest men and women on the Forbes 400 grew out of one original founder selling his original wares or services, to one customer at a time.

There's long-standing debate over selling as art or science, as creative performance or mechanical process; as talent or skill, even as something requiring of genetic predisposition.

To business owners and corporate leaders, it is too often an isolated function; to the savviest, part of an integrated process; to a few, only a necessary evil.

To those of us who appreciate it as one might appreciate art, it is, done masterfully, a thing of beauty to be admired—and rewarded; that's why some of the best customers are or were, themselves, sales professionals. To others, to consumers who've been treated badly, to critics, it's something quite ugly, to be feared and loathed.

To the economy, it is the most essential lifeblood. If the economy were required to subsist only on consumer spending done entirely of consumers' and businesses' own initiative, only of basic necessities, the entire world would come to an end in damn short order. We can certainly survive a few months of all politicians on vacation, all lawyers on vacation, all teachers on vacation, and just about everybody else but the doctors who cope with our health emergencies and the police, fire, rescue, and military troops who safeguard our lives here and abroad on vacation. But we couldn't survive even a month with all salespeople on vacation. America would be in a Depression that would make 1929 look like a day at Disney World faster than a mouse-click, and the rest of the world would follow us off that cliff. Like it or not, if no salespeople sell today, *nobody* eats by next week. And every day, every journalist and entertainer supported by ads sold by salespeople, stocks and partnership investments sold by salespeople, the ads and investments made possible by other salespeople selling every imaginable thing, every one of them should publicly give a prayer of thanks to salespeople. Every day, every politician blithely spending money that is not his and wealth not even yet created, should get down on bended knee and thank America's salespeople. It is something to be proud of.

To some of us, it is all these things and more. It is a way of life. A source of independence, self-reliance, security. A way of being of service. Even a state of mind.

However you define it and describe it for yourself, it is important. As something important, it deserves your best efforts. It should be done well or you should not do it at all, go find something else to do, and leave it in the hands of those who will do it justice. My intent for this book, above all other motives, not the least of which is to sell something (in case you hadn't noticed), is to help you do selling justice.

HOW TO READ
ANYONE'S MIND

Note: This small book was originally written for a private corporate client in 1993. It has been out-of-print for quite some time. I've been told used copies have changed hands on eBay for as much as $360.00. As I said earlier, I have made very minor changes to it mandated by time; however it is reprinted here 90% as it was in original edition.

If you have an especially strong interest in this subject, I would also recommend another book to you, which was sent to me by one of my longtime Members, a professional magician, Dave Dee. It is a book titled *The Full Facts Book of Cold Reading*, subtitled "a comprehensive guide to the most persuasive psychological manipulation technique in the world and its application to psychic readings." It is a detailed inside look at how professional psychics elicit information and do what are called cold readings of people. If you cannot find this in bookstores, try the author's website, www.ianrowland.com. I found it fascinating, accurately based on what I already knew, and valuable, enhancing techniques I use.

• • •

HOW TO READ ANYONE'S MIND

Subvert Your Own Ego

Boy, are we vain! And, at the drop of a nickel, we'll be into the "can you top this game" with anybody we're talking with. If the other person has an "I was so drunk" story, we've got a better one—if the other person has a sexual conquest story involving twins, we've got to trot out ours involving triplets. And, when we legitimately know more about something than the other person, we are compelled to demonstrate that superior knowledge.

This tendency must be suppressed if you are intent on learning as much as possible about a person from a particular conversation.

The Ego is the enemy of communication anyway. The perfect path to another's trust is the suppression of your ego, so that his may shine.

The Easiest Way to Get Anybody to Confide in You Like Their Most Trusted Friend, Fast

There is a classic persuasive marketing principle: people want most what they get the least of. And what most people get the least of is recognition, appreciation. This is true of the most successful person you know as it is of the most "ordinary" person you know. At all levels of achievement, people are starved for recognition and appreciation. You can open a person up like magic, by dispensing lots of these two things.

For example, the busiest person in the world will back off from his "busyness," will have all his calls held, will drop whatever he's doing to spend time with you and tell you everything you can think of asking—if you're very, very appreciative of how busy and important he is, of the time he makes for you.

When a person gives you some information, if you demonstrate appreciation for it and recognition of its value, guess what? He'll be eager to give more. I get a lot of free consulting and help from otherwise high-priced, busy experts with this strategy. I'll say something like: "You know, just that piece of information, that story's worth the price of lunch. I'm going to be able to use that . . ." and I'll describe the value the information has for me. What does this prompt? More disclosure. With this approach, I can get CEOs telling me their life stories and disclosing all the details of their businesses and finances in short order.

Keep in mind that everybody loves giving advice. Asking people for their opinions and their advice is a certain way to open a person up and get him "spilling" what he knows.

How to Ask Questions

1. Ask questions that cannot be answered "yes" or "no."
2. Preface with "What do you think about . . .?" or "how do you feel about . . . ?"
3. Form an extension question by repeating key words. For example:

   Wife: "You seem preoccupied. Is anything wrong?"

   Husband: "No."

   Wife: "There must be something."

   Husband: "Just a little trouble with the boss."

   Wife: "Trouble with the boss?"

4. Start with questions that are easy to answer.

5. Exchange information—don't relentlessly interrogate.

6. Stimulate further disclosure by agreeing when you can.

Study Good Interviewers

Here's your opportunity to watch television with a purpose. Many talk show hosts are very skilled interviewers, adept at getting their guests to "reveal themselves." Barbara Walters, Dick Cavett, Johnny Carson, Larry King, and Oprah Winfrey are exceptionally talented interviewers.

When you watch these and other hosts/interviewers, take note of the things they do repetitively and consistently. Look for the skill behind the style, the thing that is done so consistently it must be "principle."

Determine That You Will Learn Something from Everybody

This is an attitude that is particularly useful in getting information from others—a firm conviction that there is something to be learned from everyone and a determination to learn something from everyone.

As with most things, attitude is at least as important as aptitude, if not more important. This simple mind-set will draw people to you and motivate them to open up to you.

Listening Skills

You probably know, the inability to listen accurately and effectively costs this country billions and billions of dollars annually. There are big problems—defense contractor cost overruns, airplane crashes, all sorts of mistakes made in business and industry—because while one person insists he said it right, it was heard wrong. There are little productivity problems, too. And business and personal relationship destruction. And students' poor grades. And on and on—all because, while enormous investments are made throughout childhood and adult life to teach us how to speak and how to write, very little is done to teach us how to listen.

I read a very interesting article years ago, where a number of professional prostitutes were interviewed, and many said that many of their "regulars" often paid not for sex, didn't even have sex, but for someone to listen to them. Just recently, I saw a *Geraldo* show with operators of 900-number/800-number "phone sex" businesses, and they said the same thing—many regulars call and do not engage in explicit sex talk but instead talk about the day they had, their frustrations at work or at home, etc.—they pay for someone who will listen to them. This is just one of many situations that has convinced me that REAL listening is a rarity, and therefore immensely valuable and marketable.

To listen effectively and ACTIVELY, I think you need to do all these things:

L = LIKE

You have to find some thing(s) to honestly like about the other person.

I = INTEREST

You have to instantly cultivate a sincere interest, either in the other person or in the content of what the other person is saying. For example, I'll pay attention to, say, the CEO of American Airlines because of an interest in what he's saying on a talk show, because I travel a lot, and because I'm in business, not because he is a particularly interesting person; I'll pay attention to what Gregory Hines is saying on a talk show, not because I'm interested in tap dancing, but because he is an interesting, passionate person.

S = SEE

Meaning you have to really extend yourself to see the other person's point of view, to visualize the background and causes of the person's thinking . . . . to use your mind's eye for greater understanding.

T = TOUCH

Meaning you have to let yourself be "touched" and, as the phone company says, "reach out and touch" the other person; let there be emotional linkage. If you try to keep yourself distant and uninvolved, the other person will sense it, respond by mirroring, and crawl into a protective shell.

E = ENGAGE

Take some initiative and be actively involved, without taking away control from the other person. Display your involvement by nodding, posture, other body language, brief questions, agreement when possible, non-offensive devil's advocate type questions.

N = NEED

You've probably heard the phrase "need to know," as in—"we'll tell them on a 'need to know' basis." I suggest operating on a NEED to know basis; you have such a thriving, thirsty curiosity about what makes people tick that you really need to know as much about other people as you need to breathe. This creates clearly sincere enthusiasm for what others tell you, encouraging them to tell you more.

ACTIVE LISTENING means that, overall, you are as involved in a conversation as the person doing most of the talking. Leaning forward, nodding, appropriate facial expressions, in business setting taking notes, all help. The most important part of all, though, is "total concentration."

To be able to totally concentrate, you have to first do what the *Psycho-Cybernetics* author Dr. Maxwell Maltz called "clearing the calculator." Most little hand-held calculators have to be "cleared" of one problem before working on another. You have to do this mentally. You may use meditation, self-hypnosis, the Silva Method, whatever. But there is nothing more flattering or compelling than totally concentrating on another person's personality.

The Technique of "Displayed Interest"

Every one of us has, at least once, had the experience of meeting and spending time with someone who displayed such rapt fascination with us that we wound up telling them the most amazing things about ourselves . . . we so enjoyed being with them we sought to prolong the meeting. Many times, this is courtship behavior. We fall in love with the person of the opposite sex who seems to be unendingly fascinated with us!

I was reminded of this not long ago, when meeting with the owner of a public relations firm that I was considering hiring. She was fascinated with me. She was so focused on me a bomb could have gone off without disturbing her concentration. I was completely captivated by her nonverbal flattery. It was only after the meeting that I logically analyzed what had just happened, how I'd been mesmerized, how I'd wound up talking so much about me.

It's this kind of Displayed Interest that can get people to tell you everything about themselves.

I Will Never Forget . . .

. . . a young lady I knew only as a business acquaintance whipping out one of her newly remodeled breasts for my inspection. What could provoke such behavior? In thinking it over afterward, I'm convinced it was nothing more (or less) than my being an extraordinarily good listener, to a person desperate for attention and consideration. It is only one of many, I think amazing incidents that have happened to me while practicing the art and science of listening.

Most people go through their daily lives with others only "surface listening" to them. I experience this constantly myself and so do you. People ask us how things are going or how we are, without wanting to know or waiting to hear anything more than a "fine" or "okay." Most people "listen" while doing other things—walking, shuffling paper, whatever. At home, dinner conversation is replaced by the TV trays in front of the tube, and I'm guilty of it too. After a period of time of this, a person becomes remarkably vulnerable to anybody who stops, digs in, and really listens. A great cause of unhappiness in many peoples' lives is the absence of anyone who is thoroughly fascinated with them and what they're all about. Filling this void gives you access, even control.

What Does "Reading Between the Lines" Really Mean?

You've heard the phrase—"you have to read between the lines"—but what does that really mean? When a person talks or writes, he *communicates two ways at the same time*; with EXPLICIT messages and IMPLICIT messages. Explicit is the actual, as-stated message. Implicit is the "extra message" implied by voice inflection, body language, punctuation, etc.

Just as an example, has someone ever said to you, "If I were you, I would . . . " Or, has someone said, "I don't care where we go for lunch. Chinese would be great, but I'm up for anything." In both cases, there is an implicit or extra message quite different from the explicit message. And, in both cases, there is an attempt at manipulative control. In the first example, the person really means: here's what to do. In the second, the person really wants Chinese.

Discipline yourself to ALWAYS listen for the implicit or extra message.

Incidentally, the less secure a person is, in general or in a particular situation, the more likely he'll communicate his true thoughts through these extra messages rather than his exact words.

Eye Contact

At conventions or trade shows I sometimes catch myself committing this "communication sin"—carrying on a conversation with one person while frequently glancing around, watching for other people I know and need to talk to. Maybe it's forgivable in the trade show environment, but it's still discourteous to the other person and, more importantly, a huge impediment to total communication.

Maintaining total, unwavering eye contact with the other person gives you incredible power. This is another aspect of active listening, of displayed interest, of flattery, all of which contributes to the other person's desire to confide in you. Also, because "the eyes are the windows to the soul," you gain an intuitive sense of the other person via the eye contact.

Body Language

You probably remember "body language" as kind of a business fad. For a while, everybody was writing about body language, everybody was talking about body language. It was "hot." Then the business public moved its attention to the next panacea and it was pretty much forgotten. If you find a book on body language at the bookstore today, it'll be buried on a bottom shelf with dust on it.

However, it's as valid as ever.

We communicate much more, much more openly nonverbally than we do verbally. Even while our lips lie, our physical movements tell the truth. (Some people have a real problem with their facial expressions and other physical movement matching what they're saying so that, while others may not realize it consciously, it makes them uncomfortable subconsciously, so that they do not trust that person.)

There are two ways to use an understanding of body language. One is in the reading of others' minds. How do you tell when the person across the desk has "bought" your idea? If there are ten women at the bar, how do you tell which one is eager to be asked to dance? If you're a speaker, and there are 20 people in the front row, how can you tell which one is alone? In an office setting, how can you determine when someone is really "in a good mood," to approach them with your idea or request?

The second use of an understanding of body language is in reinforcing and empowering your own verbal communication. You can first make sure that your physical movements and facial expressions are congruent with what you're saying and how you're saying it. You can go beyond that and make your physicality communicate on a level by itself. There are masters at this. If you watch the *Personal Power/Tony Robbins* TV infomercial with the sound turned off, you'll still pick up a certain positive, intriguing energy from Tony throughout the show, but if you watch many other people being interviewed (regrettably, myself included) that doesn't shine through. Glenn Turner has a particular body movement he makes during the course of a motivational speech, hooked to an especially compelling and persuasive point, that draws the audience's attention, pulls them toward him, actually moves them to the edges of their seats.

In one-on-one selling, I've learned there's a physical "way" that communicates neediness to the other person, and drives away sales. There's a different physical "way" that communicates complete dispassion about whether or not the sale gets made, that draws sales in. For want of a better way to describe it, the relaxed body language wins every time.

NO B.S. **Sales Success** 🏵 225

In Johnny Carson's closing broadcast, he brought a stool out on stage and sat down on the stool, to talk to the studio audience and viewers at home—I think the first time he had ever sat down on a stool on stage. Why did he do that? By doing that he instantly and more effectively communicated: "Tonight is very different and very special, and I'm going to deal with it and you differently, more intimately than ever before. I'm not going to talk at you; I'm going to share with you" than if he had said all that a hundred times over.

If you want to end a conversation, you can hasten the other person along with certain body language. If you don't mind annoying the other person, looking at your watch is the blatant version of this.

We can convey what's on our minds and discover what's on others' minds with body language, and I suggest blowing the dust off the old body language books and making a fresh study of all this to be a very useful thing to do.

Mirroring

Tony Robbins has "popularized" this, but it's not anything new. The Amazing Kreskin, a mind-reader by profession, wrote this, back in 1984:

> The ideal rapport is a mirror image of those you're confronting. Let them see their best selves in you. If you're talking to someone who's bombastic, be pleasantly bombastic, but not competitive. If the person is shy and soft-spoken, reflect that tone in yourself . . . there's a little of everyone else inside each of us, and the challenge is to find what in us is in tune with the other person and reflect it.

Each of us has a particular way of speaking, a cadence, a speed, a vocabulary. Most of us appreciate a particular kind of

BONUS BOOK / HOW TO READ ANYONE'S MIND

humor—we don't necessarily laugh at the same jokes that our neighbor does. Being in tune means reflecting these aspects of the other person.

Even your physical presence can enhance or detract from rapport. I'm quick to remove the tie and jacket and roll up shirt sleeves the instant I sense my audience is in a casual mood . . .

I study the person's gestures. Does he use his hands a lot? I do too. If not, then I won't either.

Simply, people accept, trust, and spill their guts to people who they see themselves in. I've often done very well with hugely successful, entrepreneurial men who created their success out of dust, struggled, failed, recovered, made it through hard work and hustle—because they see themselves in me. Conversely, I have a rough time dealing with corporate, middle management bureaucrats who've gone from college to corporate environment, and are better at office politics than anything else—because they cannot see any of them reflected in me. But, when you really understand this, you can identify some "thing" about just about everybody you can mirror.

Humor, mentioned by Kreskin, is a great mirroring opportunity. Recently, I was the odd man out, the new dynamic in a group of five people who had already been working together, been at several meetings together, and, although they were not in sync themselves, their corporate-political tendency would be and was to unite in fear and resistance against the "outsider." As I sat there that morning, hoping for an opportunity to create rapport with somebody, the fifth guy rolled into the meeting room and told everybody a joke. In this case, it was a macho, coarse, "blue" joke, a locker-room joke. This told me a lot about that guy. Among other things, I decided to be a little "earthy" in my language, particularly when agreeing with or piggybacking on this guy's comments. It wasn't long before he "bought me," became my ally, nodded approvingly when I made a point.

I'll tell you something very interesting about all this, hopefully in a way that is not offensive to anybody. I have a number of friends in the hair styling/hair salon industry, including a lady I've been friends with for many years—in fact, we dated between my marriages. Most of the men in her salon and, in my observation, in the industry, are openly gay. Women love these guys. They attach themselves to them, they confide in them, they tell them the most amazing things. We've talked about this, and everyone concludes that the reason is mirroring; these gay men mirror the women.

There's a fine line here, to be aware of. I do not suggest becoming a total chameleon, changing to match the other person like a chameleon changes colors to match his environment. That's going too far. You have to be you; there has to be a core personality that is a constant. But short of cutting into that core personality, you can learn to modify your approach, to "lean" in the same direction as the other person you're working with at the moment.

The example of speed of speaking is a good one. Slowing or accelerating your speed of speaking is certainly not the same as comprising your personality. But it can be very helpful in making the other person comfortable.

When you meet a new person for the first time, that person instantly provides a "snapshot" of what they're comfortable with—their speed of speaking, their posture, their gestures—and you can immediately make some modifications in yourself, to mirror the other fellow. I think of it as about a 20% adjustment— 80% of me stays constant, 20% tries to adapt, to mirror the other person I'm dealing with.

The Right Image

Your "outer package" does have an impact on how quickly and easily people accept you, trust you, relax with you, and reveal themselves to you.

I can tell you for a fact, for example, that chiropractors who meet with new patients dressed "like a doctor" will get farther, faster, than the chiropractor who insists on being "casual." There are occupational biases, geographic biases, all sorts of biases, and you can use them to your advantage or fight them, your choice.

Be Prepared

I'm amazed at the people who go into sales calls, negotiations, meetings, etc. wholly unprepared, either "winging it" or applying the same "canned" procedure to everybody. This is fine if you're selling a nickel-and-dime commodity, but if you're dealing in the "Important," it's best to be as prepared as possible.

A lot of the people I deal with have books they've written or that have been written about them, tapes, there have been magazine or newspaper articles, or I know somebody who knows them—and, before a meeting, I'll delve into as much of this as I can to get a feel for that person. For my high-priced seminars, I have attendees complete and turn in detailed questionnaires in advance, so I can get that feel for them before actually meeting them. From this kind of information, I'm often able to correctly anticipate how a particular person thinks, how they're "wired."

Observe

I like meeting with people in their environments, because their environments reveal a lot about them.

An office with a wall full of plaques and certificates says something very different compared to one with a wall full of photographs of people, doesn't it? I deal with several ex-pro athletes. One has an office virtually devoid of memorabilia from his sports career. Another has an office full of footballs, trophies, photographs of teammates, and so on. What do these two offices communicate? I initially gambled and was proved right that the first person's office says that he has decided to put all that behind him; in fact, he is eager to shed his jock past and be known for his entrepreneurial accomplishments. Talking sports with this guy is a mistake. Ignoring that entirely and zeroing in on business discussion is correct. The second fellow still clings to and relies on his on-field accomplishments and that celebrity. He is comfortable with that, still uncomfortable with the business world. Asking him for an autographed ball is the right thing to do.

There's a scene in the movie *Shining Through* where Michael Douglas asks Melanie Griffith to close her eyes and recall what she has noticed about his office. It's a good test. When you go into a new environment, challenge yourself to be so observant that you can close your eyes after a minute and recall a lot of detail about the office. Then analyze what that office has to say about its occupant.

The Chink in the Armor

Everybody, no matter how successful, has at least one "chink in the armor" and knowing about it may help you better deal with that person. Often, in fact, more often than not, it's a self-esteem related chink.

For example, I have one client and friend, a very, very successful, smart, capable businesswoman, in the top 5% income bracket in the United States, probably in the top 5% in her particular profession, and, on the surface, understandably very confident and independent. But she is remarkably "hung up" on the fact that she did not attend college. Her feelings about this "lack" inhibit her and affect her in surprising ways. There's another individual I deal with, again, in his profession enormously successful, but largely disliked by his peers, not respected by his staff, and totally taken for granted by his spouse. This guy is starved for recognition. I have a client who has gone through years of struggle, then several years of remarkable success; he is terrified that it's going to end tomorrow. Can you see how being aware of the chinks in these peoples' armor makes it easier to help them, if you're into helping them; to sell to them; to manipulate them? To predict how they will respond to a particular idea or situation?

Five Human Characteristics That Can Be Relied On; What Are People Thinking

1. Resistance to Change

Yes, people can be motivated to accept, even welcome change, but, initially, the instant reaction to any and all proposed or perceived change is resistance, for a variety of reasons, including fear, inconvenience, laziness, territorial protectiveness, etc.

2. Wandering Attention

People have limited and decreasing attention spans. They lack the ability and know-how to concentrate. Their attention can easily be attracted by anything that is pleasurable, exciting, or entertaining. The more complex the idea you are presenting, the more certain "wandering attention" is. Therefore, at any given moment, you can bet the other person is thinking about personal concerns, his to-do list, a sexual fantasy, just about anything but the subject at hand.

3. Wishful Listening

People have the uncanny ability to hear what they want to hear, not what is being said. And they'll later swear they heard what they believe they heard.

4. Jumped to Conclusions

People are impatient, so, rather than hearing another person out, they'll often mentally cut him off and make an assumption about everything he's saying.

5. Habitual Negative Thinking

Most people think mostly negative thoughts. Their first reaction will be to see the negative, the difficult, the impossible, and the unpleasant aspects of something.

When you keep in mind that these five characteristics largely control the way a person is thinking most of the time, it becomes ridiculously easy to "predict" their specific thoughts and reactions in a particular situation. If using this for persuasive purposes, you then want to prepare with all this in mind and try to control these elements rather than letting them control the outcome.

How Physical Characteristics
Affect a Person's Thinking

It's my belief that short men are more aggressive, meaner, if in power, more bullyish than tall men. Overweight men are more easily intimidated and more motivated by a desire for acceptance, recognition, and respect than men of average weight. Blonde, very attractive women are most eager to demonstrate their intellect, to be asked for their opinions on important matters. Women are much more observant than men, so a man's dress and appearance is more important when meeting with a woman than when meeting with a man. A woman wearing a lot of jewelry is easily influenced by flattery; a woman wearing little or no jewelry will be turned off by casual flattery.

All this is stored in my memory bank. I don't think about it much, consciously; in fact, I had to work at dragging it out for this book, but it is there and it does influence my behavior with these types of people.

What observations have you made about how physical characteristics are predictive of thinking and behavior?

Sure, these are generalizations, biases. And I know that they are subject to attack as over-simplifications, and certainly subject to exception. But I ask that you keep in mind that I deal in one-on-one situations, with dozens of different people each week, a thousand or so a year, and, in groups, tens of thousands more, and I believe I have sufficient evidence to draw and reasonably rely on these conclusions. And when you consider the pace most of us are on these days, the speed at which we meet, greet, interact with, and move on, the use of pigeon-holing, of quickly categorizing people, is virtually essential.

Demographic Clues to Attitudes

People born and raised in the Midwest are more trusting and trustworthy than those raised in California.

How do you feel about that statement? Sure, it's unfair. There certainly are very trustworthy people born, raised, and living in California. I have one or two such clients there myself who have the highest imaginable integrity. And certainly there are some people of zero integrity born and raised in Kansas, Indiana, and Ohio. But, setting aside the individual cases and deliberately trying to develop a generalization that is truer than false, I'd bet on this one.

Let's stay with California for a second. Image and appearance is more important there than anywhere else in the United States. People in L.A. are much more likely to quickly form very firm conclusions about you based on the car you drive, clothes you wear, and whether or not you have a portable phone than people in, say New Orleans or Indianapolis. If you're going to do business in L.A., you'd better get a grip on this.

People raised in high-income families will have very different values and opinions than people raised in low-income families. People living in major metropolitan cities respond differently than those living in small towns, to just about everything. For example, there's less cynicism in small town residents than in city dwellers. People with children—parents—certainly respond differently than do married couples who do not have children.

In marketing to groups or people, we consider their demographic commonalities. When we can, we'll deliver a very different marketing message for the same product to a group of 45-year-olds from Rhode Island than to 35-year-olds in Atlanta. And, different demographic groups are drawn to different products—for the most part, the women who regularly read *Cosmopolitan* are different than those who regularly read *Redbook*; the men who read *Playboy* different from those who read *Hustler*. Since all this applies to marketing to groups, why wouldn't it apply to influencing individuals?

I try to get a "demographic profile" in my mind of the person I'm working with—what are his "vital statistics"?—age, income, marital and family status, home town, educational background, etc. I ask myself: who else do I know who closely matches that demographic profile? What is that person like?

I happen to know a guy very, very well who is the demographic clone of H. Ross Perot. They both got their early entrepreneurial experience delivering newspapers on horseback. Their upbringing—virtually identical. I mean, their backgrounds are virtually interchangeable. As a result, watching Perot-the-candidate come forward was especially interesting to me. I know what Perot's going to say before he says it. When Marilyn Quayle attacked him on the *Today Show*, I knew instantly how Perot would react and what he'd say. There's a technical term for this: "demographic overlay." If you can do a demographic overlay, you can quickly read someone's mind.

The Biggest Difference: "Think" vs "Feel"

There is a substantial amount of very good, very interesting, and very sophisticated literature out there about the importance of communicating differently with men than with women, and you can make a study of all this if you like. But the shorthand, shortcut is that most (not all) males respond primarily on a "thinking" level; most (not all) women respond primarily on a "feeling" level . . . e.g., "how do you feel about that" vs. "what do you think about that?"

If you want to achieve open communication, making this single adjustment and staying on the appropriate think/feel "channel" is very important.

I'd add that women generally, and probably correctly, trust their "intuition," instincts, subconscious mind's opinions, whatever you want to call it, much more than men do. Whether they ever analytically sort it out or not, women seem more tuned into non-verbal communication, to confidence; they've got better built-in truth detectors than we do. (Except when "blinded" in a romantic relationship.)

Be an Informed, Interesting Person

You have to be able to talk with people about what interests them before you can get them to open up to you.

I once built a very good relationship with a banker by getting involved with his obsession with fly-fishing. I didn't know a damned thing about fishing when we met, but when I discovered the incredible commitment he had to his hobby, I went and got educated very quickly.

As a general rule, the more you know about a broad, diverse range of "stuff," the better. I have a client who loves horse racing—it so happens, I know a lot about horse racing, so, as Joan Rivers says, "we can talk." I have another client who's very into the theater. Before I visit with her, I make sure to get a copy of *The New Yorker* and the Sunday *New York Times*, to get caught up on what's going on in the theater, so "we can talk." I have a client who is very involved with . . . well, you get the idea. I suppose in any given month, I read dozens of trade magazines, dozens of specialty magazines, I watch TV programs dealing with subjects of interest to a client, and so on.

I want to be informative AND entertaining. Compare the salaries of Jay Leno with a college dean, by the way, and you'll instantly know which of the two is most important.

How to Know When a Person's Resistance Is Irrational

The signs of irrational opposition are:

1. VEHEMENCE. If a person expresses his disagreement with more intensity and excitement than the situation seems to warrant, he's lost control. He may even be fighting an internal battle that has nothing much to do with you.
2. STONE-WALLING. If a person is unresponsive, refuses to discuss or debate or ask questions.
3. IRRELEVANCE. If a person introduces irrelevant arguments, goes off on tangents.
4. OBJECTION PING-PONG. If a person introduces an objection, has it answered, trots out another objection, then another after it's answered, then another.
5. PARANOIA. If a person trots out a collection of "worst case scenarios."

When these "signs" occur, know that any attempt at logical persuasion will be thwarted. Your choices are a) to extricate yourself, retreat and return to persuade another day, or b) risk confronting the person about his behavior and asking for the real, hidden reasons for the resistance.

It is, incidentally, almost impossible to change the mind of "the true believer." He uses all five of these to keep himself linked to the chosen belief. If you want to understand his unshakeability and/or you are involved in creating "believers," i.e., members, customers, recruits, etc., THE book to get and study is Eric Hoffer's *The True Believer*. This book explains everything from

David Duke, Ross Perot, etc. to Amway to Tim and Tammy Bakker.

F.O.R.M.

I teach this to people involved in multilevel network marketing, as the process for breaking the ice with strangers, getting conversations going, and very quickly finding out what's most important to a person . . . but it'll work for anybody, not just a network marketer.

FORM is an acronym, to help you remember the four things to ask everybody about.

F—STANDS FOR **FAMILY**

For some people, family is THE most important thing in their life, and the path to fast rapport is ooh-ing and aah-ing over the snapshots of kids and grandkids.

O—STANDS FOR **OCCCUPATION**

For many people, their business or career is either their greatest area of pain or greatest area of joy, and expressing interest in that is like turning on a faucet.

R—STANDS FOR **RECREATION**

Some people live for their hobbies. Golfers, fishermen, and photographers, for example, are rabid about these activities.

M—STANDS FOR **MONEY**

A lot of people are extremely interested in everything related to money. If they see an art object in your home, they can't help but wonder what you paid for it. I'll always remember being in an adult nightclub (topless dancing establishment) with a group of entrepreneurs, noticing that the most successful guy had wandered off, and finding him back in the dressing (or "undressing") room, sitting, surrounded by mostly naked, attractive women, studiously asking questions about gross sales, average tab, tips, and other financial statistics.

Each individual is more interested in one of these areas of life than the other three. Once you isolate which one a person is most interested in, you can often accurately predict what he's thinking in response to certain stimulus.

For example, take four guys hearing a news item about a very successful baseball player's new contract. "F" thinks: my kid's got an arm like a rocket. I hope he grows up and makes the majors. "O" thinks: what a dumb job, running around playing a kid's game. "R" thinks: oughta get some of the guys together and play some ball this weekend. "M" thinks: geez, two mill a year! I wonder how much that works out to, each time at bat?

Similarly, when you make ANY statement, the other person "processes" it "through" his primary interest in life, family, occupation, recreation, or money.

The Power of Suggestion

Some people bought this book not out of a desire to "read" others' minds but, instead, to "control' others' minds. Without passing judgment, let me tell you that, to a great degree, you can do exactly that, if that is your chief aim. To control a GROUP of people, study Eric Hoffer's book *The True Believer*. Probably without intending to, he provided a very practical, precise method for gaining control over a room full or a nation full of people.

To control or direct an individual's thoughts, rely on the single power of suggestion. For starters, lock this principle into your mind: people translate the words they hear into pictures, think in pictures, and are most readily led by pictures.

If I say to you, "If you die, will you leave your family penniless and in poverty?" You automatically get a picture in your mind. Now that may be a classic, Depression-era picture of a woman and a couple urchins, in scruffy clothes, sitting on a doorstep. It might be a gleeful picture of your cheating, bitching, ungrateful wife bursting into tears at the reading of your will. It will be a picture, but I have exerted little control over what the picture will be. I could further suggest the nature of the picture, couldn't I? And that's the "trick"—to deliberately extend the suggestion.

If I say: "Let's take a week off and go to a beach somewhere" I'm again leaving the picture at risk. You may conjure up a positive, persuasive scene of you on a beach, getting a tan, watching gorgeous girls in skimpy bikinis, etc.—or you may pull up the very memorable picture of your last trip to Mexico, sunburn, stomach virus, and all. But if I fully detail my picture, I can make it your picture. If I say: "Let's take a week off, go to the beach, get a couple of hammocks in good positions, a cooler of drinks, some good books, leave the cell phones locked up at home and really relax . . . and I know just the place, where there'll be a good breeze, pure white sand, clear water, and lots of great-looking women . . ." What pictures are you forming in your mind now?

Try this exercise. Find a quiet, comfortable place to sit. Sit down and clear your mind as best you can. Now think back to the last time you took a good, bracing hot shower—maybe this morning—and concentrate on your fingers and hands, the hot water splashing over them. Switch to starting and building a fire. See yourself rubbing your hands together over that great fire, soaking in the warmth.

It won't be long before your hands actually get warmer. The power of suggestion is so great that most people can raise or lower their entire body temperature or any part of their body by 10 to 15 degrees purely through mental imagery. There is a physiological reaction to a psychological exercise.

Cavett Robert said "people won't buy burial plots unless they see the hearse parked at the door." He oughta know—he made a fortune teaching people how to sell burial insurance. And the key word there is *"see."* So your job is to speak in a way that conveys the right pictures. Know that everything you say will become pictures—the question is: what pictures?

When I say, from the front of the room in my marketing seminars, "Think about what it would be like to get up each and every morning KNOWING, absolutely knowing, exactly how many calls you will receive that day, from new prospects ready and eager to do business with you. What would that feel like? How would you like to live that way?" I'm hoping for some very definite pictures . . . that the person in the audience sees himself, getting up spryly, eagerly, rather than crawling out of bed; smiling into the mirror; maybe answering the phone and getting a pleasant call from a customer. But whenever time permits, I go ahead and add: "I'll bet you'd get out of bed a little differently than you do some mornings now. I'll bet you'd jump up and say 'Good morning, God!' instead of 'Good God, it's morning.' I'll bet you'd give that mirror a big smile." This is suggestion at work.

Now, any good hypnotist or hypno-therapist will tell you that some people are more "suggestible" than others, so this works differently with different people. And it's rare that anybody gets so good at using the power of suggestion that he can literally, totally control another person's responses. But make no mistake about it, everybody has some degree of receptivity to this type of suggestion, and anybody can learn to use this power.

Essential Reading

Bodybusiness by Ken Cooper, AMACOM

Getting Through to People by Jesse Nirenberg, Reward Books

Secrets of the Amazing Kreskin by Kreskin, Prometheus Books

Use Both Sides of Your Brain by Tony Buzan, Plume Books

Unlimited Power by Tony Robbins, Fawcett

The True Believer by Eric Hoffer, Dimension

Summary of Key Strategies

1. Don't "show off." Let the other person have the spotlight. Subvert your ego.

2. Give lots of recognition and appreciation.

3. Show appreciation for the value of the information given to you by the other person.

4. Build the other person up—ADD to his/her self-esteem.

5. Be a cheerful person.

6. Maintain a healthy sense of humor.

7. Avoid the "feel" of interrogation.

8. Reveal yourself (to get others to reveal themselves).

9. Learn to creatively structure your questions.

10. Emulate others who ask questions effectively.

11. Have the "learner" attitude.

12. Listen ACTIVELY.

13. Totally concentrate.

14. SHOW your interest.

15. Realize what a great emotional need just about everybody has to be listened to.

16. Be alert for the "extra messages."

17. Maintain eye contact.

18. Learn to read body language.

19. Learn to "speak" body language.

20. Use specific body language to set up and assist special communication situations. (Johnny Carson example.)

21. Learn to "mirror."

22. Present the most effective image.

23. Prepare.

24. Invade the other person's environment and be observant. (Thinking leaves clues.)

25. Look for the chink in the armor.

26. Play the odds. Bet that basic human characteristics are at work.

27. You CAN judge a book by its cover.

28. Consider the person's demographics.

29. Motivate women differently than men and vice versa.

30. Use "FORM" to discover the person's main area of interest.

31. Know a little about a lot of different things.

32. Think twice about trying to accomplish anything with a person who is clearly irrational.

33. Use the power of suggestion.

PART VI

REFERENCE SECTION

ABOUT THE AUTHOR

D AN S. KENNEDY is a multimillionaire serial entrepreneur; influential author, and popular profession- al speaker; strategic advisor, consultant, and business coach—and above all else, a salesman since he could talk and until his last breath. In addition to his business activities, he is on the advisory board of The School of Communications at High Point University, and writes a weekly column on politics and business published at BusinessAndMedia.org and syndicated to numerous newspapers and popular political blogs. He resides, with his wife, Carla, and The Million Dollar Dog in Ohio and in Virginia, and drives professionally in harness–horse races at Northfield Park near Cleveland, Ohio, over 100 times a year. Inquiries concerning his availability for speaking engagements or consulting assignments, or comments or correspondence about this book, should be directed by fax to (602) 269–3113.

Other Books by the Author

No B.S. Business Success for the New Economy, Entrepreneur Press

No B.S. Marketing to the Affluent, Entrepreneur Press

No B.S. Wealth Attraction for Entrepreneurs, Entrepreneur Press

No B.S. Direct Marketing for Non–Direct Marketing Businesses, Entrepreneur Press

No B.S. Time Management for Entrepreneurs, Entrepreneur Press

Ultimate Sales Letter, Adams Media

Ultimate Marketing Plan, Adams Media

Websites with Additional Information from the Author

www.NoBSBooks.com

www.DanKennedy.com

www.RenegadeMillionaire.com

•

ETERNAL TRUTHS

Dan Kennedy's
#1 No B.S. Truth About Selling

If you're going to achieve high levels of
success in selling, you've got to
be able to get positive results
under negative circumstances.

• • •

Dan Kennedy's
#2 No B.S. Truth About Selling

You don't have to be a psychic to read
someone's mind—he or she will read it out
loud to you, with a little encouragement!

• • •

Dan Kennedy's
#3 No B.S. Truth About Selling

It's a good idea to learn from other people's
experience, but usually with this caveat: seek
out and learn from those with experience
who are at the top of their game.

• • •

Dan Kennedy's
#4 No B.S. Truth About Selling

The logic is simple: if the packaging of products has an impact on how people regard those products, then the packaging of people must have an impact on how others regard those people.

• • •

Dan Kennedy's
#5 No B.S. Truth About Selling

A top performer in selling is always focused on selling. He or she takes this attitude, described by Zig Ziglar: you've got my money in your pocket and I've got your product in my briefcase, and I ain't leaving until we make the exchange.

• • •

Dan Kennedy's
#6 No B.S. Truth About Selling

Super–successful salespeople expect successful results.

• • •

Dan Kennedy's
#7 No B.S. Truth About Selling

What others say about you and your product, service, or business is at least 1,000 times more convincing than what you say, even if you are 2,000 times more eloquent.

• • •

Dan Kennedy's
#8 No B.S. Truth About Selling

In persuading others to part with their
money, your best possible approach is
demonstrating that the apparent expense
is not an actual expense at all; that the
thing being purchased is either free or,
better yet, actually pays.

• • •

Dan Kennedy's
#9 No B.S. Truth About Selling

If you're going to arrive at the sales
presentation that achieves the maximum
possible results, you're going to have to test a
lot of different things that disappoint along the way.

• • •

Dan Kennedy's
#10 No B.S. Truth About Selling

Your financial success will be very closely
related to your ability to minimize your time
spent meeting with people not qualified and
ready to buy, and to maximize your time
spent face–to–face with people who are
qualified and ready to buy.

• • •

Dan Kennedy's
#11 No B.S. Truth About Selling

Prospecting sucks.

• • •

Dan Kennedy's
#12 No B.S. Truth About Selling

When have you ever heard of anybody
going to see the wise man at the
BOTTOM of the mountain?

•   •   •

Index

- Two CDs Of The **EXCLUSIVE GOLD AUDIO INTERVIEWS**

  These are EXCLUSIVE interviews with <u>successful users of direct response advertising, leading experts and entrepreneurs in direct marketing, and famous business authors and speakers</u>. Use them to turn commuting hours into "POWER Thinking" hours.

* The New Member No B.S.® Income Explosion Guide & CD (Value = $29.97)

This resource is <u>especially designed for NEW MEMBERS</u> to show them HOW they can join the thousands of Established Members **creating exciting sales and PROFIT growth** in their Business, Practices, or Sales Careers & Greater SUCCESS in their Business lives.

Income Explosion FAST START Tele-Seminar with Dan Kennedy, Bill Glazer, and Lee Milteer (Value = $97.00)

Attend from the privacy and comfort of your home or office…hear a DYNAMIC discussion <u>of Key Advertising, Marketing, Promotion, Entrepreneurial & Phenomenon strategies</u>, PLUS answers to the most Frequently Asked Questions about these Strategies

* You'll also get these Exclusive "Members Only" Perks:

- **Special FREE Gold Member CALL-IN TIMES:** Several times a year, Dan & I schedule Gold-Member ONLY Call-In times
- **Gold Member RESTRICTED ACCESS WEBSITE**: Past issues of the *No B.S.® Marketing Letter*, articles, special news, etc.
- **Continually Updated MILLION DOLLAR RESOURCE DIRECTORY** with Contacts and Resources Dan & his clients use.

  To activate your MOST INCREDIBLE FREE GIFT EVER you only pay a one-time charge of $19.95 (or $39.95 for Int'l subscribers) to cover postage (this is for everything). **After your 2-Month FREE test-drive, you will automatically continue at the <u>lowest</u> Gold Member price of $49.97 per month ($59.97 outside North America). Should you decide to cancel your membership, you can do so at any time by calling Glazer-Kennedy Insider's Circle™ at 410-825-8600 or faxing a cancellation note to 410-825-3301 (Monday through Friday 9am – 5pm). Remember, your credit card will NOT be charged the low monthly membership fee until the beginning of the 3rd month, which means you will receive 2 full issues to read, test, and profit from all of the powerful techniques and strategies you get from being an Insider's Circle Gold Member. And of course, it's impossible for you to lose, because if you don't absolutely LOVE everything you get, you can simply cancel your membership before the third month and never get billed a single penny for membership.**

EMAIL REQUIRED IN ORDER TO NOTIFY YOU ABOUT THE GLAZER-KENNEDY UNIVERSITY WEBINARS AND FAST START TELESEMINAR

Name _____ Business Name _____

Address _____

City _____ State _____ Zip _____ e-mail* _____

Phone _____ Fax _____

Credit Card Instructions to Cover $19.95 for Shipping & Handling:

_____Visa _____MasterCard _____ American Express _____ Discover

Credit Card Number _____ Exp. Date _____

Signature _____ Date _____

Providing this information constitutes your permission for Glazer-Kennedy Insider's Circle™ to contact you regarding related information via mail, e-mail, fax, and phone.

FAX BACK TO 410-825-3301
Or mail to: 401 Jefferson Ave., Towson, MD 21286
www.In12Months.com